D0132358

GLOUCESTER MASSACHUSETTS

Whole Health

for happy cats

**A GUIDE TO KEEPING YOUR CAT
NATURALLY HEALTHY,
HAPPY, AND WELL-FED**

QUARRY BOOKS

Sandy Arora

Foreword by Regina Schwabe, DVM

First published in the United States of America by
Quarry Books, a member of
Quayside Publishing Group
33 Commercial Street
Gloucester, Massachusetts 01930-5089
Telephone: (978) 282-9590
Fax: (978) 283-2742
www.rockpub.com

Library of Congress Cataloging-in-Publication Data
  Arora, Sandy.
  Whole health for happy cats : a guide to keeping your cat naturally healthy, happy, and well-fed / Sandy Arora.
        p.   cm.
  Includes bibliographical references and index.
  ISBN-13: 978-1-59253-266-7 (pbk.)
  ISBN-10: 1-59253-266-7 (pbk.)
  1. Cats. 2. Cats—Health. 3. Cats—Diseases--Alternative treatment. 4. Holistic veterinary medicine. I. Title.
  SF447.A76 2006
  636.8083—dc22   2006010361
                                                                                                          CIP

ISBN-13: 978-1-59253-266-7
ISBN-10: 1-59253-266-7

10 9 8 7 6 5 4

Design: Richard Oriolo
Layout: Leslie Haimes
Cover design: Rockport Publishers
Cover image: Wothe/www.jupiterimages.com
Illustrations: Colleen Hanlon

Homeopathic treatment is best done under the guidance of a homeopathic veterinarian. Neither the author nor the publisher, Quayside Publishing Group, accept liability for any mental, financial, or physical harm that arises from following the advice or techniques or consuming or using the products and procedures in this book.

For my wonderful husband, John,
and my darling cat, Boo Boo,
without whom I would never have realized
my love for cats.
They are both responsible for
bringing out the crazy cat lady inside me.

Contents

Foreword

Cats play a unique role in our lives. They're our companions and help connect us to nature at a time when that connection has weakened because of modernization and urbanization. They also serve as sentinels, alerting us to toxins and deficiencies in our environments and lifestyles before we're aware of their effects on us. In health and illness, they have much to teach us.

No other domestic animal is as sensitive to change as the cat—the canary in the coalmine of our modern environment. Domestic cats have high cancer rates, chronic disease, and immunodeficiency in spite of increased indoor living, plentiful food, and limited exposure to infectious agents and parasites. Our cats should do so much better than their ill-fed, diseased, and wild-living feral counterparts. Feral cats do have a much shorter lifespan—one year, if we factor in kitten mortality and accidents—whereas domestic cats live fourteen years on average, with many reaching eighteen or nineteen years. However, domestic cats rarely reach the age of ten without developing at least one chronic illness. Commonplace ailments include hyperthyroidism, heart disease, chronic renal disease, chronic cystitis, diabetes, inflammatory bowel disease (IBD), skin disease, and cancer.

What do we need to do for our cats to help prevent these problems? This book strives to answer that question. We know some of the answers already, and we'll know more in the future. Some of these insights can even help us with our own health.

We know that diet plays a huge role in health. In the 1960s, the readily available high-carbohydrate, grain-based cat foods resulted in an increase in dilated cardiomyopathy, diabetes, pancreatitis, IBD, obesity, and hyperthyroidism in cats. Nowadays, a species-appropriate diet that meets the highly specialized cat's essential needs can help prevent these health problems. We've also discovered the connection between potassium deficiency and certain neurological conditions, taurine deficiency and congestive heart failure, and high-glycemic index foods and diabetes.

Cats have also drawn attention to the potentially adverse effects of overvaccination by developing fibrosarcomas at the sites of certain injections. This directly led to a look at vaccine protocols and recommendations to increase intervals between vaccines. We also know that cats react sensitively to drugs of all kinds, even those that many other species can safely take. For instance, aspirin and essential oils in potpourri can poison cats.

Cats have shown us that, to do no harm, you must first thoroughly understand each individual's needs. Everyone—cat or human—is born with a vital energy that can only thrive in the proper context and order. Our cats depend upon us to choose the healthiest lifestyles for them.

To do that, we have to think like a cat. A domestic cat's short list of needs includes peaceful and clean surroundings; opportunities to play and exercise; and a nutrient-rich, meat-based diet. Even more important, chemical-sensitive cats need protection from unnecessarily harsh and invasive treatments and drugs. In this book, you'll learn about some gentle homeopathic, herbal, and traditional remedies you can safely use for your cat. We can tap this long tradition of what North America and Europe call alternative medicine—traditional medicine to 80 percent of the world—on behalf of our cats.

This book mainly emphasizes prevention. To prevent disease, we try to make environmental and dietary choices that support the vital energy to the body. Obvious requirements include proper light, fresh air, and clean water (without chemical additives) as well as exercise, stimulation of the senses, and food that nourishes without harming. But meeting these requirements requires some effort. Our water, for example, is a chemical soup that contains small amounts of such ingredients as drugs, pesticides, and herbicides. Our foods grow in nutrient-poor, chemically-enhanced soil that robs them of nutrition; they're also full of hormone-like substances that can affect metabolism and organ function. We can't control many of these problems, but we need to do our best with what we currently know. We know that proper diet and environment promote health. We know a few vaccines prevent fatal disease, but overvaccination can cause chronic disease. We know wellness checks can help detect problems before they become major, but many treatments cause further deterioration of the immune function.

By taking an active interest in preventive care and healthy lifestyles for our cats, we contribute to our own self-awareness. If we respect and support the delicate balance that is health in our feline companions, then we can begin to work on ourselves and our environment. Above all, we are more willing to assume responsibility for our own health and well-being once we've seen how it helps our wonderful cats.

—Regina Schwabe, DVM
    Pamplin, Virginia

Introduction

"There is no such thing as 'just a cat.' "

ROBERT HEINLEIN

Cats are said to have nine lives. Because they're independent, they're often viewed as tough, when in reality they're anything but. This misconception, coupled with a tendency for cats to hide their illnesses so they won't be seen as weak, has resulted in a lack of appreciation of cats' needs for care. As a highly refined predator, a cat has a finely tuned physiology that's easily thrown out of balance. As guardians of our cats, we should strive to provide them with optimal nutrition and healthcare, using safe and holistic methods.

I became involved in the study of natural cat care when my beloved Boo Boo was diagnosed with kidney failure and hypertrophic cardiomyopathy. Although he was given only six weeks to live, alternative methods kept him happy and comfortable for twenty months. Inspired by my experience, I established Holisticat, an online discussion list—and later a companion website—devoted to nutrition and alternative health care for cats. I've written *Whole Health for Happy Cats* as part of my quest to make holistic cat care available to everyone, particularly those who don't have the time to weed through a daunting number of books, journals, and Internet sites to glean the vital information they need to make informed decisions about their cat's health.

Part One of this book focuses on prevention: the key to whole health. Part Two tackles physical and emotional health. If you provide your cat with wellness checkups, a healthy diet, and natural care, you'll minimize the need for at-home care as well as expensive and frequently invasive veterinarian treatments for such conditions as bladder inflammation, bowel conditions, allergies, dandruff, and so on. If your cat does develop one of these conditions, general good health will make it more likely that your cat will recover. By avoiding excessive vaccinations, drugs, and chemicals and instead choosing good nutrition, flower essences, herbs, and homeopathy, you can naturally make your cat's life longer, healthier, and happier. What greater joy could there be for a cat lover?

Cats are unique. Foods, medicines, supplements, and other substances that can help humans and other animals can seriously harm cats. This book is filled with tips, recipes, and remedies for cats, that you can whip up in a matter of minutes with everyday ingredients found at home. Each recommendation results from research (and in some cases, practice) to account for cats' unique nutritional needs. A resource guide at the end of the book and checklists interspersed throughout provide quick references for supplies needed for routine care and minor ailments. And, although each chapter builds on information from previous chapters, feel comfortable using individual chapters and appendices as quick and ready references.

I have supported hundreds of cat caregivers since 1997 in their quest to prevent and cure disease and provide good nutrition. As a college professor, I've used my training in research methodology to translate publicly available research findings into terms everyone can understand and use. I've enjoyed this labor of love for years, and I hope the knowledge I've gained through my study and correspondence will help you keep your cats healthy so you can enjoy their love and companionship for years to come.

Part One: Prevention

This book takes a prevention-oriented approach to cat care. Taking care of a cat should be fun, not work. This book will give you easy, inexpensive, and safe solutions for everyday cat care and for dealing with minor ailments. Holistic care and judicious use of herbs and other natural remedies will go a long way to keep your cat's coat soft and shiny, her eyes bright and clear, and her spirits high. Caring for the whole cat involves feeding a species-appropriate diet of fresh, raw meat free from fillers, chemicals, and preservatives and offering appropriate supplements. You can complement this diet by making sure your cat receives only minimal vaccinations and by maintaining a toxin-free home. Then, just mix in equal parts of love and affection and your happy, healthy cat will reach her full potential.

CHAPTER ONE

The Basics of Holistic Cat Care

"Happy owner, happy cat.

Indifferent owner, reclusive cat."

CHINESE PROVERB

Cats are very clean creatures and have a well-earned reputation for fastidious self-care. But even the most meticulous and independent cats can't take care of all their basic care needs; they need you. And if you approach regular care sessions with love and a positive attitude, not only will grooming and tending to your cat be fun for you both, but you'll also always know your cat's overall state of health and be able to detect early warning signs of developing problems.

Which Dish Is Best?

When selecting feeding dishes, ask yourself these questions:

- **Is the material safe for cats?**
- **Is it microwave-safe?**
- **Will it stay in place while my cat eats?**
- **Can I wash it in the dishwasher or in water hot enough to kill bacteria and viruses?**

Happy Cat Necessities

Before you bring your cat home, go shopping so that you'll have all your cat's essentials ready and waiting. You'll need food and water dishes, litter, one or more litter boxes, toys, a scratching post, and grooming supplies. Stock your kitchen and natural medicine cupboard with supplies that are safe for all feline and human members of the household.

Ceramic bowls guard your cat against allergy and skin problems associated with plastic.

Food and Water Dishes

The most important items your cat will need are water bowls and one or more food bowls. When selecting dishes, their shape and what they're made of is more important than aesthetics. Most cats, especially those with flatter faces such as Persians, prefer eating from plates rather than from bowls because bowls flatten their whiskers and keep them from reaching in far enough to eat all the little bits of food. So choose a shallow bowl or small plate, and look for one at least five inches (13 cm) across so your cat can reach food easily without smashing her whiskers along the side.

Avoid plastic dishes because cats can develop allergy and skin problems from regular exposure to them. The most common problem plastic dishes cause is feline acne, which appears as black specks on a cat's chin. Some cats also develop contact dermatitis, which only gets worse from continued exposure to plastic. Plastic also tends to nick and scratch, and all those tiny nicks can harbor bacteria and become a breeding ground for germs, including those that contribute to feline acne. Finally, if your cat likes warm food, keep in mind that plastic doesn't microwave well.

For a multi-cat home, choose a flat-bottomed water bowl and several food dishes.

The safest choices for bowls and plates are ceramic, stainless steel, or glass. Glass is microwavable and dishwasher safe, but it's also breakable. Stainless steel, while not microwaveable, is sturdy and dish-

> Add hot water to your cats' food to release its aroma, making it more palatable, particularly for those with appetite problems.

washer-safe. Keep in mind that some decorative plates and crystal bowls, although quite beautiful, contain lead. Over time, tiny fissures in these bowls can allow lead to leak out, even if the dish passed lead inspection when new. As a safeguard, turn the plate or bowl over to check for lead-free glaze.

If your cat tries to drink water from the faucet, it means she prefers running water to still water from her bowl. Consider getting your cat a water fountain so she'll always have fresh, filtered, simulated running water. Not only does ample water intake ensure your cat stays in good health, it also makes her happy by giving her something that pleases her.

Litter Boxes

A litter box's depth should be just right for your cat— if it's too shallow, litter might fly about when your cat digs in her box. If it's too deep, she may have trouble stepping into it.

Place your cat's litter box in a quiet, peaceful place that provides some privacy. Make sure your cat has easy access to the litter box, but don't place it close to the feeding area. Some cats don't like covered litter boxes, so experiment as needed. Keep in mind that your cat will more likely use a litter box that's easy to access and use. When you select a litter box, decide how many boxes you'll need, the size and style of the boxes, and whether you want self-cleaning boxes.

NUMBER OF BOXES

Given the cleanliness of cats, conventional wisdom suggests one litter box per cat, plus one extra. If you have a small living area or many cats, make sure you have at least half as many litter boxes as you have cats. To cut down on litter box odor, sprinkle a thin layer of baking soda on the bottom of the box before pouring in the litter.

SIZE AND STYLE

Your cat should have a litter box large enough to stand in comfortably and turn around. Any shallow plastic storage container or large baking pan can work as a litter box. Some cats like covered pans because it gives them more privacy. However, some cats find a covered box somewhat confining and won't accept it. Most average-sized cats—seven to eight pounds (3.2 to 3.6 kg)—do fine with a small litter box, but bigger cats sometimes prefer a roomier box. Jumbo litter pans or large plastic storage containers work well for bigger cats. For older cats or those that have trouble getting into and out of a pan, a shallow litter box works best. Use a small saw or utility knife to cut an opening in the front of a pan to allow your older cat easy access.

Covered litter boxes are good for humans, too, because they contain carbon filters that help control odor.

SELF-CLEANING

Self-cleaning boxes are a good option for cat lovers who want to provide their cats with a clean box at all times. Self-cleaning boxes, which require scoopable litter, contain a mechanical arm that sweeps across the box and scoops litter ten minutes after it detects movement. My online mailing list, Holisticat, has received mixed reports, with positive reviews from cat caregivers with just one or two cats but some negative reviews from those who live with many cats. Reports mention some difficulty cleaning the waste storage compartment and potential problems if a male cat urinates too close to the litter box mechanism, which may cause mechanical problems.

A soft mat or carpet placed at the spot where your cat exits her litter box will prevent her from tracking litter around the house.

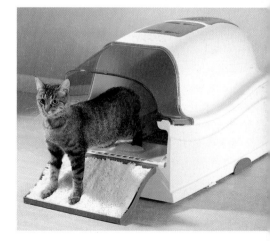

Whether you use a covered or uncovered box, mechanized box or basic pan, above all, keep the litter boxes clean. You can clean the area around the boxes with a diluted vinegar and water solution. This also cuts down on odor in the general litter box area. A mix of baking soda and water removes lingering odors and leaves litter boxes clean. You can use a mild liquid Castille soap to wash out litter boxes each week. A ten-to-one solution of water and regular household bleach makes a good disinfectant. Never use ammonia with bleach; this can release chlorine gas, which can burn the eyes, nose, mouth, and respiratory tract.

Litter

The first decision to make when purchasing litter is whether to buy clumping litter or pellets. Clumping litter, or scoopable litter as it's sometimes called, needs less frequent replacement but requires you to scoop stool and urine clumps each day. With pellets, you can just remove the solid waste each day (no urine clumps to scoop) and shake the tray to make the sawdust settle toward the bottom of the pan. However, you'll need to dump out the whole box and start over every two to four days, depending on usage.

Some anecdotal evidence indicates that clumping clay litter is dangerous if ingested, particularly by kittens. Fortunately, several safer types of clumping litter now exist. These choices continue to grow and currently include corn, wheat, paper, pine, and cedar. So if you choose clumping litter, you'll next have to decide what material you and your cats prefer.

Why Isn't My Cat Using Her Litter Box?

Location Issues:

- **Nearby foot traffic or household appliance use may make it too noisy.**
- **The room it's in may have an unpleasant odor.**
- **If you recently moved the litter box to a new area, your cat might not like the change.**

Litter Box Issues:

- **A covered box may feel constricting.**
- **The box may not be clean enough.**
- **Too many cats may share one box.**
- **Your cat may have trouble accessing it if it has high sides or is in a spot your cat can't easily navigate.**

Litter Issues:

- **The litter may be too heavily scented or have a scent your cat doesn't like.**
- **It may not feel good on her paws (this can sometimes happen with wood pellets or silica-based crystals).**

Health Issues:

- **Your cat may have a urinary tract infection (UTI) that causes pain during urination, causing her to associate the litter box with pain.**
- **A cat with a UTI, which can cause a constant urge to urinate, may not make it to the litter box in time.**

Multiple cats in a household can make the litter choice difficult, as all cats may not like the same type of litter or box. You may need to provide two or three types of litter as well as a variety of boxes to keep all your felines happy.

Avoid pine or cedar shavings sold as bedding for small animals because these contain phenols, a chemical compound that can irritate your cats' paws and lungs. Wood pellets are safe because they have no additives, based on Environmental Protection Agency guidelines. Also, kiln drying has already released the harmful phenols in pine and other aromatic woods, making these soft wood litters safe for cats.

Cat Litter Options for the Budget Conscious

Wood stove pellets: Compressed soft wood pellets manufactured for use in wood stoves cost very little. These wood stove pellets have the same properties as wood litter products marketed for cats except that they tend to be larger. You can introduce wood stove pellets by mixing a small amount into the wood litter you currently use then slowly increase the amount. Buy only soft woods; you can find them in hardware or feed stores that sell horse bedding.

Chicken feed crumbles: If your cats prefer clumping litter, you can buy nonmedicated chicken feed crumbles—also known as chicken scratch or mash layena—at pet feed stores. Because it costs so little, you can fill each litter box with only an inch or two and dump the crumbles the next day. Or you can use it to line the bottom of the litter pan before adding clumping nonclay litter. This option works particularly well for kittens because eating crumbles isn't as dangerous for them as eating clay, although alfatoxin from mold can be a concern with any grown litter. As your cats dig in the box, the crumble mixes with the regular litter, so either use a fifty-fifty ratio, or experiment as you see fit. Make sure the crumbles have a short ingredients list, with corn as the primary ingredient, and that they don't contain any additives.

Clay

■ The most commonly available litter, clay isn't particularly absorbent and requires daily scooping of solid matter. Because liquid waste stays in the litter, the litter requires weekly replacement.

■ costs little
■ readily available
■ causes no adverse effects

■ doesn't control litter box odor
■ some, although not excessive, tracking
■ not ideal for cats with diabetes or kidney failure

Clumping or Scoopable

■ Besides sand, clumping litter options include ground corn, wheat, paper, and cedar litters, all of which form clumps with varying degrees of hardness.

■ controls odor
■ flushable (except for septic systems)
■ requires less frequent replacement
■ includes safer, nonclay options such as corn, wheat, paper, and cedar

■ causes tracking (a mat next to the pan can help control this)
■ may be ingested by kittens (higher risk with clay litter)
■ some nonclay litters don't clump as well

Paper Pellets

■ Paper pellet litters absorb liquid and swell in size. They require daily removal of solid waste and weekly changing.

■ absorbs liquid and odor
■ benefits the environment because it's made from recycled paper

■ can smell a bit soggy
■ needs weekly replacement
■ can track if not replaced promptly
■ can be expensive

Wood Pellets

■ A byproduct of the furniture industry, wood pellets are made from compressed sawdust of soft woods, such as pine. They require daily removal of solid waste and replacement once or twice a week.

■ initially causes very little tracking
■ absorbs odor
■ benefits the environment because it's a recycled product

■ if not changed quickly enough, it tracks (if it's mostly at the sawdust stage)
■ may feel unpleasant to some cats' feet

Crystals

■ Litters made from nontoxic silica beads and crystals are lightweight and last longer than clay litter. You only need to scoop out solid waste each time while stirring the crystals to keep the urine from pooling at the bottom of the pan. You will need to purchase a special scoop, as crystals are too large to filter through a regular scoop.

■ biodegradable
■ no dust
■ flushable
■ controls odor
■ not much tracking

■ noisy when cats dig
■ can be expensive, especially with multiple cats
■ some cats don't like the feel of it on their paws
■ not advisable for cats with diabetes or kidney problems, because it doesn't perform as well when there is excessive urine in the box.

Make Your Own Odor and Stain Remover

This very effective cleaner is an inexpensive alternative to the ones available at pet stores. Since it involves mixing baking soda and hydrogen peroxide, don't shake or cap it, or you risk an explosion. But don't let that deter you from using it; just be careful. Always test this solution in an inconspicuous area first before trying it on a more prominent place in your home. Don't let it sit out for more than half an hour or the hydrogen peroxide will lose its effectiveness; it's best to mix it up fresh each time just before use, and then rinse out the mixing container. Mix this solution in a glass container to avoid any chemical reactions.

INGREDIENTS

8 ounces (235 ml) of 3 percent hydrogen peroxide

1 drop dishwashing liquid

1 teaspoon (5 g) baking soda

INSTRUCTIONS

Combine the ingredients in a glass container using a wooden spoon. Pour the contents into a handheld carpet-cleaning machine, and use it the way you would any cleaner to thoroughly clean stained and smelly carpet sections. Rinse out the machine's cleanser compartment immediately. If you don't have a carpet cleaner, just liberally apply the solution to all stained and smelly areas. For a particularly soiled area, sop up some solution with cloth or paper towel and then reapply it; you don't need to blot it. Once the area dries, you shouldn't see the stain or notice the smell any more.

Clean minor stains as soon as possible with a mixture of 3 teaspoons (15 ml) vinegar, 1/2 teaspoon (2.5 ml) dish liquid, and 2 cups (475 ml) water. When dry, apply baking soda liberally and vacuum the next day.

Scratching Posts

Cats have a natural tendency to scratch. Placing several scratching posts around the house will give your cat the proper outlet for her scratching needs. Because cats love climbing trees and perches, buy a post with at least one tall ledge, and make sure you buy posts at least two feet (0.6 m) high. If you get a taller post, make sure it's sturdy and stable. A lot of posts have carpet covering, which may emit formaldehyde. If you can't avoid using carpet-covered scratching posts, place them in a well-ventilated area until the smell dissipates.

A tall scratching post allows your cat to satisfy her need for scratching and stretching.

To discourage your cat from scratching carpets in the house, don't use carpet-covered posts, or you may confuse her. Sisal, a reasonably priced material, has a texture cats usually love and lets them really sink their claws into it the way they can sink their paws into tree bark. You can make sisal posts at home by covering any wooden structure with sisal; use a staple or hot glue gun to attach the sisal.

Some people even bring real tree bark home for their cats to scratch. Another cat favorite is a piece of plywood covered with burlap; once the burlap shreds, you can easily and inexpensively replace it.

If your cat likes to scratch on carpets or other horizontal surfaces, you can try catnip-treated corrugated cardboard, available at pet supply stores at a reasonable price. Some of these have a string on top that lets you hang it from a door, or you can just lay it flat on the ground for your cat to scratch and sometimes even sleep on. The more a cat scratches, the more catnip the cardboard releases, so cats love both the aroma and the texture of these cardboard scratchers. You can refresh the cardboard by sprinkling catnip on it from time to time.

A horizontal scratching post made from material other than carpet may keep your cat from scratching carpets in the house.

Toys provide hours of mental and physical stimulation for your feline companion.

Happy Cat Necessities

food dish

water dish

nail clippers

brushes, combs, and fur clippers

child-sized toothbrush or gauze

litter scoop

litter pan

litter pan liners

scratching pads or posts

toys

beds or cardboard boxes

Toys

Playing with cats and watching them play is such a joy. Of course, spending a lot of money on cat toys doesn't guarantee your cats will accept them. Quite often, cats prefer the box the toy came in. One solution is to make homemade toys. You can just wad up some aluminum foil or paper for them to bat around. Some cats also love pouncing on cotton swabs and plastic rings from milk jugs. If a cat spots a pen or pencil on a table, she'll have a hard time resisting the urge to bat it down to the floor.

Some cats are mousers and prefer toys they can drag along the floor; others prefer birdlike objects that flutter or fly. You'll notice a difference in your cat's interest level based on whether she prefers hunting birds or mice. Of course, some versatile cats love both, so be prepared to buy or make lots of different types of toys.

Cats also love to play and sleep in paper grocery sacks and small cardboard boxes. If your cats don't play with each other or on their own, try creating simple interactive toys, such as a shoelace tied to a wooden dowel or a metal rod. The possibilities are endless, but be careful; a cat can accidentally ingest a small toy in the heat of play. Some cats like to chew on strings, tinsel, and rubber bands, so either keep them away from your cats altogether or supervise at all times to

prevent choking. Cats are also drawn to plastic bags because they're sprayed with animal fat. Unfortunately, some cats like to chew on the plastic, which can block their intestines if they eat it. To prevent this, store plastic bags out of your cat's reach.

Basic Body Care

At least twice a month, attend to your cat's basic body care needs. Trim her nails (using a guillotine-style or a standard human nail clipper), clean her eyes and ears, and brush her teeth. Also, brush or comb your cat's coat at least twice a month to keep it healthy. Brushing distributes the oils from her body, making her coat softer and glossier. You'll have an easier time of it if you have another person there to hold the cat steady. Otherwise, hold the cat in your lap or in the crook of your left arm (if you're right-handed), with your cat's back turned away from you.

Spaw Treatment

Make the time you spend tending to your cat's body care a special bonding time. Enhance daily brushings by giving your cat a soothing massage, complemented with plant hydrosols or edible oils such as grape seed or hemp seed oil.

Perform basic body care while holding your cat in the crook of your right arm (if you're left handed) with her back away from you.

Claws

Cats' claws grow constantly, and as they grow, the outer layer of their claws sheds; it's not unusual to see these sheaths lying around scratching posts. When trimming your cats' claws, work in a well-lit area so you can see the claws clearly. Each paw has four claws, with the front ones containing an extra claw called the dewclaw.

Happy Cat Natural Medicine Kit

Begin collecting these items the day your kitty comes home, and expand your kit over time. We'll discuss loose dried herbs and herbal extracts in Part Two.

- aloe vera gel and juice without sodium benzoate
- apple cider vinegar
- chamomile
- Chinese herbal powder Yunnan Paiyao
- coenzyme Q10 (CoQ10) powder or soft gels
- colloidal silver in various concentrations: ten to forty parts per million (ppm) for internal use and one hundred to five hundred ppm for topical use
- cranberry extract with no sugar added
- decaffeinated green tea
- decaffeinated green tea powder, also called Shiki Matcha
- extra virgin olive oil
- eyebright
- grapefruit seed extract: tablets for internal use and liquid for external use
- homeopathic euphrasia tincture
- mullein leaf
- neem
- peelu bark
- pure, unrefined coconut oil or butter
- vitamin C (calcium ascorbate powder)
- vitamin E gel capsules
- stevia powder packets and liquid
- yellow dock

If your cat has an underlying health condition such as renal failure and you see sudden redness in one or both of her eyes, take her to the veterinarian; such a sign may indicate a serious problem, such as a detached retina.

Examine your cat's paws when she is relaxing in your lap. Start with gentle stroking, eventually pressing gently on her paw pad to reveal her claws.

Cats have retractable claws that you can extend by pivoting the end bone of the toe over the tip of the next bone. When you gently squeeze the middle of your cat's paw with your nondominant hand, the claws will unsheathe and extend from the paw pads. With your other hand, clip the pointed ends of the white portion of the claw. The quick refers to the pink tissue close to the base of the paw. If you accidentally clip into this part, it will bleed. Keep the Chinese remedy Yunnan Paiyao close at hand; a few grains of this applied to the claw will stop the bleeding, reduce any swelling, and help the claw heal. This powder is available online and at Asian herb shops. If you don't have access to Yunnan Paiyao, you can use stevia liquid extract instead. You can dab it directly from the bottle on the bleeding area. If you can't get either Yunnan Paiyao or stevia liquid extract, use powdered cinnamon, although it's not as effective.

Eyes

Your cat should have clear eyes, with no discharge. Some cats are prone to a watery discharge that results from problems with their tear ducts. When their tears come into contact with air, the oxidation causes the discharge to turn reddish brown.

Your cat's eyes should always be clear and bright. Eye problems can be very serious, so never ignore signs of injury or damage.

NATURAL EYEWASH OPTIONS

Use these recipes to clean and soothe minor eye irritation. You can apply these with a dropper, or you can soak a cotton ball in the liquid and either gently place the cotton ball over the eye so some of the liquid gets into the eye, or gently squeeze the cotton ball so one drop gets in the eye. Hold your cat gently but firmly in the crook of your elbow, and be prepared for her to make sudden, jerky head movements.

- Freshly squeezed cucumber juice: Place one drop in each eye three times a day until symptoms stop.

- Homeopathic euphrasia tincture: Place three drops of the tincture into two tablespoons (28 ml) of clean spring water. Use one to three drops of the diluted solution in the eye.

- Cod liver oil: Pierce capsule and squeeze one drop in the affected eye three times a day. Because some liquid cod liver oil supplements include flavorings, use capsules that contain only vitamins A and D.

- Colloidal silver: You can use any concentration up to 150 ppm. Apply one drop in the affected eye three times daily.

- Eyebright and chamomile infusion: Pour one cup (235 ml) boiling water over a half teaspoon of each dried herb for a total dried mix of one teaspoon (5 g) and let sit for twenty to thirty minutes. When the liquid has cooled, wash your cat's eye liberally with it. She might need several drops three to four times a day.

Your cat's ears should be clean, light pink, and healthy, with no debris, growths, odor, or discharge. Ear mites are contagious, so if you host a cat suffering from ear mites, use preventative treatment on other cats.

Ears

A healthy cat shouldn't scratch her ears frequently. If you see your cat doing this, take a peek at the skin just inside the earflap and close to the ear canal. A brown or black deposit that looks like dried coffee grounds indicates ear mites. Treat ear mites aggressively because they can lead to secondary bacterial and fungal infections. Continued redness and inflammation can set your cat up for problems down the road, so prevention and early care is the key to keeping your cat free of ear problems.

Natural Ear Wash

This ear remedy combines the antibacterial elements of garlic with the soothing properties of olive oil. You can use it to clean ears as well as smother ear mites. Minor ear infections sometimes respond to this treatment, but for more serious infestations, consult your veterinarian.

INGREDIENTS

2 cloves fresh garlic

2 tablespoons (30 ml) olive oil

2 cups (475 ml) water

3 drops oil from a vitamin E soft gel

1 drop grapefruit seed extract

INSTRUCTIONS

Chop the fresh garlic, place in a small bowl, and add enough olive oil to cover the garlic. Place the bowl over some just-boiled water, or heat it in the microwave for thirty seconds. Unless you need it immediately, let this infusion sit for five to seven days in the refrigerator (or on the counter in cooler weather) so the garlic can release its medicinal constituents into the olive oil. When ready to use, strain the oil and add three drops of vitamin E and one drop of grapefruit seed extract. This mix should last up to three months if you store it in a cool, dry place. Use grapefruit seed extract very sparingly because more than a couple of drops mixed into this liquid can burn the skin.

APPLICATION

To clean your cat's ears, dab some garlic-infused olive oil onto a cotton ball, lift the earflap, and gently wipe the inside of the ears. With an eyedropper, put two or three drops as close to the ear canal as possible, let go of the earflap, and gently massage from the outside. This oil mix will help dissolve wax and prevent ear infections.

EAR INFECTIONS

If untreated, ear infections can have very serious consequences. Symptoms of an ear infection include redness, inflammation, and discharge. Discharges can range from watery to a thick, yeastlike discharge. Infections can also cause swollen lymph glands and tenderness in the ear and neck area. If your cat has severe symptoms, don't attempt to treat her at home. But if you catch this problem early on when your cat has only mild symptoms, first clean out her ears thoroughly with the garlic-infused olive oil mixture. You can also use colloidal silver 100 ppm externally as an ear wash or internally using an eyedropper.

Fungal infections can be stubborn and difficult to treat because they don't respond to antibiotics. Common symptoms of yeast infections in the ear include a musty smell and yellow or light brown discharge. An acid-alkaline imbalance can cause fungal or yeast infections; to correct this, wash your cat's ears with equal parts apple cider vinegar and water. To treat fungal infections, keep the ears as dry as possible so the bacteria don't have a warm, moist environment to grow in. If your cats will accept it, you can give them two to three tablespoons (28 to 43 g) of plain yogurt each day. Look for the ingredients Lactobacillus bulgaricus or Streptococcus thermophilus or the phrase "contains live cultures" on the carton. If your cats don't like yogurt, they can take lactobacillus supplements. Look for a product that contains several bacteria strains, such as Lactobacillus acidophilus and Bifidobacterium bifidum as well as at least one billion organisms per capsule.

You may come across toothpaste recipes containing diluted grapefruit seed extract, neem powder or extract, myrrh extract, and propolis tincture. Although these are safe and even beneficial, they taste bitter, and grapefruit seed extract may burn sensitive gums. Safer options include extracts of cranberry, chamomile, and decaffeinated green tea.

Teeth

At six months of age, adult cats will have thirty teeth. Kittens begin to grow their milk teeth at around four weeks of age. At around twelve to thirty weeks of age, kittens begin to lose their baby teeth and their permanent teeth begin to develop. By the time they're three months old, cats have twenty-six teeth with no molars.

Efficient predators, cats have teeth designed to rip and tear. To that end, they have six small incisors in the front portion of their upper and lower jaw. A large canine tooth referred to as a fang flanks both the upper and lower sets of incisors. These four fangs are what cats use to rip and tear the flesh of a prey animal. They don't have flat-crowned teeth designed to chew food. In the back of their mouths they have ten premolars and four molar teeth. Their teeth don't meet when they close their mouths. Cats lack the side-to-side grinding action human jaws have.

Cats that have lost some or even all their teeth can still manage to eat. Preventative care, such as teeth brushing and proper nutrition in the form of raw meaty bones, should keep your cat's teeth and gums in good shape.

DISEASE PREVENTION

One of the first signs of periodontal disease is inflammation of the gums, or gingivitis. A common dental problem in cats, it results from bacteria, plaque, and tartar. It shows up as reddened gums or a red line of inflammation where the gum meets the teeth. It occurs when plaque deposits build up on the surface of the teeth and beneath or along the gums. As plaque

deposits build, they harden into tartar or calculus. Once calculus forms, brushing won't remove it; it must be scraped off. As tartar builds up, it enlarges the pocket between the tooth and the gum. This enlarged pocket traps debris and sets the stage for continued bacterial growth.

Signs of periodontal infection include bad breath, gingivitis, and mouth odor. When you take your cat to the veterinarian, the doctor will clean above and below the gum line and remove calculus. However, if your cat has advanced disease, she may need surgery or extractions. To prevent teeth problems, get your cat used to teeth brushing at an early age and continue regular brushing throughout her life.

Daily brushing is the key to keeping plaque from building up at the gum line. Cats are prone to developing painful lesions or cavities at the gum line, known as feline oral resorptive lesions (FORLs). Although some evidence suggests that excessive vitamin D in the diet might contribute to FORLs, we don't know what causes some cats and not others to be prone to FORLs. The most common treatment for FORLs is extracting the affected tooth. You can perform a check at home to see if your cat has a FORL by placing a cotton swab at the gum line and pressing gently. If your cat has a painful lesion, she'll chatter her jaw. If your cat indicates any pain or sensitivity or if you see bleeding, have her teeth checked out as soon as possible.

As if FORLs weren't serious enough, cats also face the risk that harmful bacteria from infected teeth could make their way into the bloodstream through blood vessels in and around the roots of the teeth. These bacteria travel through the body and tend to do the most damage to cats' heart valves and kidneys. Such damage has been implicated in both kidney failure as well as heart valve damage. That's why keeping cats' teeth clean is so important. Regular teeth cleanings help prevent plaque forma-

tion, especially if you do not feed your cats raw meaty bones, which naturally help to clean teeth.

CLEANING

The first step to making your cat comfortable with tooth brushing is to get her used to you handling her mouth. Start by lifting the lip and gently massaging her gums and teeth with your fingers. Repeat this for several days, and keep each session short. Choose times when your cat is calm and happy, and keep your attitude upbeat, giving lots of praise throughout the session.

Once your cat is comfortable with a gum massage, move on to gently rubbing the outside of the pre-molars, molars, and fangs (where maximum tartar buildup occurs) with a piece of soft muslin cloth or microfiber dipped in colloidal silver, a solution that kills germs and bacteria. If your cat doesn't cooperate, use six-inch (15.2 cm) long, cotton-tipped wooden swabs, available in the pharmacy section of most drugstores. You can dip them into colloidal silver and get a better angle when you attempt to clean the sides of your cat's mouth or molars.

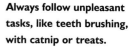

Always follow unpleasant tasks, like teeth brushing, with catnip or treats.

Even cleaning just one tooth the first time is enough to get your cat used to the idea. Immediately follow with lots of cuddles, praise, and the requisite treats. If you can't use gauze to clean your cat's teeth, use a commercially available finger brush, which has a nubby texture that helps remove plague and massage the gums. It's easier to use than a full-size toothbrush because it fits onto your finger and gives you better motion control. Eventually, you can move up to a child's soft-bristle toothbrush to clean your cat's teeth.

> **For some fungal ear infections, you can try the oral herbal supplement acidophilus, a probiotic that will help replenish the good bacteria in your cat's digestive tract.**

Tooth Powder

This powder contains ingredients research has shown to help improve teeth and gum problems. Because your cat will ingest these ingredients during cleaning, use the smallest amount possible to clean her teeth. You can use the powder daily for teeth cleaning and massaging over your cat's gums.

INGREDIENTS	6 teaspoons (30 g) green tea powder, also called Shiki Matcha; you can get decaffeinated green tea leaves and powder it using a coffee grinder
	3 teaspoons (15 g) peelu bark powder
	1 teaspoon (5 g) stevia powder
	1/4 teaspoon (1.2 g) vitamin C; use calcium ascorbate powder (not ascorbic acid, which damages tooth enamel)
	10 to 30 ppm of colloidal silver, as needed

INSTRUCTIONS

Mix all the dry ingredients thoroughly. To use, pour out 1/2 teaspoon (2.5 g) into a small plate. Moisten gauze, a microfiber cloth, or a finger brush with some colloidal silver, dip it into the powder, and rub it over your cat's gums and teeth. If you don't have access to all of these ingredients, any one or a combination will work. The powder keeps up to six months in an airtight jar.

Toothpaste

Because of its consistency, you may have an easier time using toothpaste than powder. You can add 1 tablespoon (9 g) of tooth powder to this mix. You'll need to make a batch of the tooth powder first to use in this recipe.

INGREDIENTS	10 CoQ10 soft gels
	1 to 2 teaspoons (5 to 10 ml) colloidal silver (10 ppm to 30 ppm)
	3 drops cranberry extract
	3 drops decaffeinated green tea extract
	1 tablespoon (15 g) tooth powder

INSTRUCTIONS

Mix all ingredients together and store in a cool, dry place. Apply to your cat's teeth and gums using a finger brush, piece of gauze, or a child-size toothbrush. You might notice differences in texture depending on the brands you use, so add a little extra colloidal silver if you want to make the paste moister, or add more tooth powder to make the paste less watery. The paste will last a week to ten days in the refrigerator.

Grooming

Cats with short hair need frequent combing or brushing only during shedding season (late spring through summer), but long-haired cats need frequent brushing year-round. Not only will this keep your house free of fur, it will prevent hairballs. Grooming is a great opportunity to check your cat's body for any lumps, growths, or skin problems. A word of caution about touching a cat with skin lesions: it might be ringworm, which is highly contagious. (See page 36 for more on ringworm.)

The earlier in your cat's life you start grooming her, the more used to it she'll become. Start slowly, and use it as an opportunity to bond with your cat. Speak soothingly in low tones, and start with the cheeks and chin—most cats like being scratched there and so are more likely to accept combing. If you can, scratch your cat's chin with your nondominant hand while moving on to the chest area with your other hand. Keep coming back to the face or any other area your cat likes being combed just to reinforce that brushing is a pleasant activity. As always, treats afterward go over well with any cat.

Brushes and Tools

Test any cat brush or comb first on yourself to make sure it won't hurt your cat's skin or pull on her fur, causing pain. A medium-toothed metal or Teflon-coated comb works well on short- and medium-haired cats because it won't pull or get caught in fine fur. A rubber brush made of soft material is also a good choice because it moulds to cats' bodies and is wonderful for getting out loose fur without pulling.

If you use a rubber brush during winter months, brush gently so you don't create static problems.

Brush your long-haired cat daily. Long-haired cats do best with slicker brushes that contain both long and short bristles. The long bristles go deeper into the coat to get out loose fur close to the skin, and the shorter ones remove flyaway fur closer to the surface. When buying a slicker brush, look for one with a soft, foam-cushioned pad at the base of the bristles. For stubborn mats or knots, don't ever add water because it makes removing the mat harder. You can massage some cold-pressed grape seed oil into the knot, after which you can use a mat breaker to gently go over the knot. Use a mat breaker, which typically has six stainless steel blades, only to work on matted areas; for allover combing, use a medium-toothed comb or natural bristle brush.

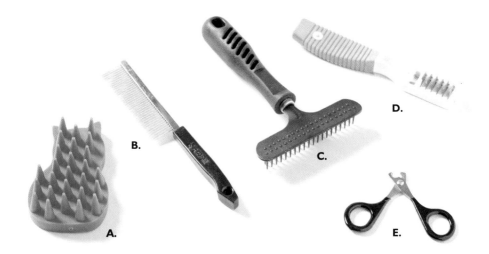

A. This soft rubber comb is called a "Zoom Groom." B. Medium-toothed metal comb helps remove loose fur without tugging. C. A brush with medium and wide teeth reaches the undercoat to loosen fur. D. When using a mat breaker, hold the fur close to your cat's skin to prevent pulling. E. Guillotine-style nail clippers are available at pet stores, but regular nail clippers also work well.

If you can't brush your long-haired cat daily, consider shaving her; then follow up with weekly maintenance brushing.

Skin Conditions

Even with regular brushing and grooming, cats commonly develop skin conditions because of lifestyle and weather changes. Skin issues in cats can range from dull, greasy fur to itching, dandruff, fur loss, and ringworm. A healthy diet combined with wild salmon oil supplements should take care of most skin problems. When general skin problems occur, straight apple cider vinegar or vinegar diluted fifty-fifty with water is a simple home remedy. Apply directly to the affected area using a cotton ball, and allow the vinegar to dry.

Several diseases have early warning signs that show up in cats' fur. For example, cats with kidney failure, hyperthyroidism, and diabetes frequently have dull, greasy fur. If your cats, especially senior cats, experience these symptoms, contact your veterinarian.

Dandruff

Cats can get dandruff when they don't have enough essential fatty acids in their diets. If your cats are prone to dandruff, you can add wild salmon oil as well as ground flax seed to their food each day.

Flax seed doesn't satisfy a cat's need for essential fatty acids; to meet their omega-3 fatty acid requirement, cats need fish body oil.

Flax seed is available in both ground and seed form. Once ground, flax seed goes rancid very quickly, so it's best to purchase seeds and use a coffee grinder to grind a few days' worth at a time and then store it in an airtight container in the refrigerator.

Longhaired cats often need more fat in their diets and frequent brushing to keep their coats soft and fluffy.

Hair Loss

Hair loss can result from physical conditions, such as flea allergy dermatitis, stress, and anxiety.

It's not uncommon for cats to have flea allergies because many cats are very sensitive to the saliva the flea injects when it bites. A symptom of flea allergies is hair loss from scratching on the back above the tail as well as around the head.

Hair loss can also occur when cats groom excessively or pull out their own fur as a result of stress or anxiety. Stressful situations for cats include the addition of a new person, cat, or other animal to the household; moving; or any other change in the cat's home environment. Cats also pick up on any stress in the household, so if a person is unhappy or anxious, cats sometimes get sad, too. Chapter six provides specific strategies for coping with cats' stress through the use of flower essences and herbs, once any physical problem has been ruled out.

Ringworm

A fungal infection, ringworm is highly contagious to both cats and people. If you detect one or more bald patches on your cat's skin accompanied by scabs or scaling, take your cat to a veterinarian, who will perform a culture test to confirm a diagnosis of ringworm. The conventional treatment includes clipping, a whole body dip, and internal antifungal medication. Avoid giving your cat steroids, they can suppress the immune system and foster an environment for the fungus to thrive.

Before starting topical applications for ringworm, carefully clip the hair over the spots to expose them to air and light (ringworm thrives in dark, damp areas). Dispose of clipped hair carefully or, better yet, burn it, because it can spread the fungus. Make sure you vacuum the area where you groomed your cat. Also, frequently wash your cat's bedding and utensils, as well as floors, tiles, windowsills, and any other areas your cat comes into contact with. Use hot water and soap along with a diluted (one part bleach to ten parts water) bleach solution.

One of the most effective yet gentle ways to deal with ringworm is to topically apply undiluted, highly concentrated colloidal silver; use a concentration of 100 ppm, 150 ppm, or, better yet, 500 ppm. Apply it to the affected areas at least five to six times a day. In most cases, the ringworm should clear up in just a few days.

Another option is to apply neem herb extract to the affected areas. Alternatively, you can open up a neem herbal capsule, empty out the powder, and make a paste by mixing it with colloidal silver (100 to 500 ppm). You can easily apply this paste to the spots, and if your cat licks it off, it won't harm her. If necessary, you can add other herbs to neem, such as goldenseal and echinacea. These gentle applications work as well as, if not better than, harsh conventional treatments.

Routine preventative care will keep your cats' health on an even keel. Paying careful attention to their needs should also help you keep medical bills in check. During petting sessions, sneak in quick peeks at their eyes, ears, teeth, and general body condition.

> To help soothe the skin while waiting for the ringworm treatment to take effect, apply cooked oatmeal to the affected areas and cover your cat's body with a t-shirt.

How to Feed Kitty Right

"The only mystery about the cat is why it ever decided to become a domestic animal."

SIR COMPTON MACKENZIE

Diet is the foundation of good health. So many of the diseases that afflict our cats these days, such as allergies, urinary problems, obesity, and IBD, can be traced back to a poor diet. Cat caregivers today have many feeding options—canned food, kibble, dehydrated, and raw. Where do you begin? We advocate a raw diet for your feline friend but understand that the choice to go raw is a personal one. Therefore, besides giving detailed information on how to transition to and then ultimately feed your cat a raw diet, this book also provides important nutritional guidelines every healthy, happy cat should follow.

Did You Know?

Overweight cats who go without food can develop a serious problem called fatty liver disease. When fat cats don't eat, their bodies move fat stores to their liver so they can be used as fuel. The liver is overwhelmed with the saturation of fat and can't function effectively. Watch for signs of anorexia in any cat, but particularly in an obese one. Signs of fatty liver disease include poor appetite, vomiting, diarrhea, dehydration, and excessive salivation; in the later stages of the disease, a cat's gums and the whites of his eyes can take on a yellowish tint.

Feeding Requirements

Most cats self-regulate their feedings, but many cats need you to do this for them. You should feed your cat $2^1/_2$ percent of his body weight if he's currently at an ideal weight, and 3 percent if he's underweight. Similarly, start feeding an overweight cat just 2 percent of his body weight, and then maintain him in the $2^1/_2$ to 3 percent range. A cat weighing eight to ten pounds (3.6 to 4.5 kg) needs around two heaping tablespoons of raw food each meal (assuming two meals per day), or one to two cans of commercial food a day.

Our cats, like the Small African cat from which they descended, need to eat several small meals a day; however, it's not feasible for most cat caregivers to feed their cats so frequently. Therefore, aim for two feedings a day spaced about twelve hours apart. Kittens, however, need more frequent meals with smaller amounts per meal.

Do Kittens Need Special Food?

Once kittens are a month old, they can eat the same food as adults but in much smaller amounts. Kittens need to eat frequently—as often as six times a day—until the age of three months. Between three and six months, they should eat four to six meals per day. Once they are between six months and one year, they can eat three to four tablespoons (42 to 55 g), or 4 percent of their body weight, two or three times a day.

While some kittens can tolerate cow's milk, some can develop digestive upset from it. If a kitten—particularly an orphaned one—is in poor health, consider giving him some goat's milk yogurt. An excellent supplement for kittens is bovine colostrum (the premilk fluid produced by a cow during the first three days following the birth of the calf) because it contains antibodies that can give a kitten a healthy foundation in life. This comes in powder form and can be mixed with spring water or goat's milk. You can also add a raw egg yolk.

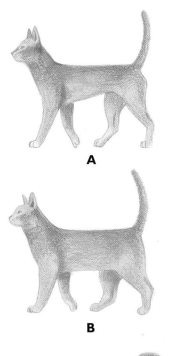

A

B

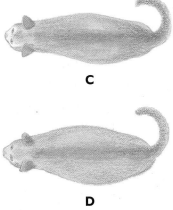

C

D

Which one of these does your cat's body most closely resemble?
A. Underweight
B. Normal weight
C. Overweight
D. Obese

Meat Jerky Treats

You can feed your cat special treats—such as dried salmon or beef and chicken livers—as between-meal snacks. The easiest way to make your own cat treats at home is to use a food dehydrator. Most food dehydrators come with at least two trays, so you can keep your cats' meat trays separate from your own trays, especially if you're a vegetarian. If you don't have a dehydrator, use a microwave with a dehydration rack.

Alternatively, you can place the meat in your oven at the lowest temperature setting, leaving the oven door slightly ajar. Place the meat strips directly on the racks or on a cookie sheet if you prefer. You can adapt these recipes to the equipment you have at home.

■ INGREDIENTS

meats: no need to use lean strips because cats have a fairly high fat requirement

chicken: breast, hearts, or thighs

beef: brisket or flank, sandwich, skirt or round steak

venison: front shoulders and cuts similar to beef

liver: chicken, pork, or lamb

■ INSTRUCTIONS

1. Slice the meat against the grain, cutting it into 1/16" to 1/8" (1.6 to 3.2 mm) strips. The thinner the slice, the more tender the final product will be, and the shorter the drying time. You can leave the strips approximately 1" (2.5 cm) wide by 6" (15 cm) long.

2. Place the meat strips in the dehydrator for six to eight hours, rotating the trays once an hour. If you want the strips crunchier, leave the meat in the dehydrator for up to twelve hours.

3. You can use the strips right after removing them from the oven or dehydrator. However, if you let the meat sit for forty-eight hours, the jerky will moisten or soften up a bit, making it easier for your cat to chew.

These jerky treats should keep for up to two years if stored in a cool, dark place. You can also freeze them and take a few out to thaw before feeding. If your cat has trouble chewing large pieces of jerky, cut them into bite-size pieces at serving time.

Nutrition

If you can't feed your cat a fresh, raw-meat–based diet, you can feed him a commercially available, grain-free brand. Cat food production has made tremendous strides over the past decade, and many reputable companies sell healthier kibble and canned food than has been available in the past.

Commercial Food

Ingredients found in many brands of kibble include corn gluten meal, brewer's rice, peanut hulls, and soy. What little meat most commercial brands contain isn't always high quality. Fortunately, some ethical commercial pet food companies now use human-grade meat; some even formulate their foods without grains. Look for a brand that doesn't contain grains and uses human-grade meat as one of the first three or four ingredients. Meat meal, a common ingredient in commercial foods, is animal tissue that has had the moisture and fat removed. Meat meal is acceptable as long as it's not the first or second ingredient on the label. You'll find recommended commercial foods listed in the Resources section, on page 170.

If you cat eats a raw diet, he won't need to eat as much as a cat who eats kibble because his food won't contain fillers, such as grains and excess fiber.

Myth Buster

Dry foods don't keep tartar problems at bay because even cats that do chew dry food, rather than swallow it whole, don't crunch long enough to provide any scraping action, particularly along the gum line. Dry food has so many negative points that even a possible small positive, such as tartar prevention, doesn't make it worth risking your cat's health.

Salmon Snacks

Salmon snacks provide your cats with the essential fatty acids found in fish. Easy to make and healthier than store-bought treats, a small tin or bag of salmon snacks makes a great gift.

NOTE: Due to content, it is best to refrigerate salmon snacks. Place small bags in the freezer for future use.

■ INGREDIENTS   YIELD: 120 TREATS

1 eight-ounce (225 g) can of salmon or mackerel with juice and bones

4 tablespoons (55 g) finely chopped fresh catnip*, basil oregano, parsley, or wheatgrass

1 finely ground eggshell

3 whole eggs, beaten well

4 tablespoons (55 g) unsalted ground pumpkin or sesame seeds

2 1/2 cups (562 g) rice* flour

■ INSTRUCTIONS

1. Preheat oven to 300°F (150°C)

2. Rinse eggshells and save the yolks and whites. Let the shells dry on a cookie sheet in the oven overnight, or bake at 375°F (190°C) for ten minutes.

3. Mix all ingredients together using your hands or a food processor until the dough is the right consistency for rolling.

4. Roll out the dough to about 1/4" to 1/2" (6 to 12 mm) thick.

5. Use 1/2" by 1-inch cookie cutters to cut in fun shapes.

6. Bake cookies at 375°F (190°C) for twenty minutes; baking for five extra minutes will make the cookies crunchier.

*In place of rice flour, you can use amaranth or quinoa flours. To make rice flour at home, pulverize short-grain rice using a coffee grinder. Grind the rice as finely as possible.

How to Pick Commercial Food

When shopping for a commercial brand of cat food, keep your cats' overall nutritional needs in mind. Adequate water intake is an important component of cats' diets, but most don't drink enough water to satisfy their nutritional needs, making it even more important to ensure your cats' diet contains human-grade meat, preferably moist canned food.

Cats' prey on animals containing a lot of moisture (70 percent or more in some cases) so in the wild, cats obtain most of their moisture needs from their food sources. Kibble typically contains around 10 percent moisture and is made primarily from grains that don't contain the correct amino acids. This makes dry food very unnatural for cats to eat. The low-moisture content of kibble means cats must drink copious amounts of water to compensate for it not being in their food. Cats don't have a strong thirst mechanism and usually won't drink anywhere near enough water while on a dry diet. This taxes their kidneys, causing cats to produce more highly concentrated urine than they would on a fresh, raw diet. Dry food can predispose cats to urinary crystals or stones and renal failure, not just because of the lower moisture content, but also from the urine-alkalizing effect of grains in kibble. Other negative consequences of feeding dry food include obesity, digestive problems (including food allergies), and diabetes.

Far superior to dry food, canned or wet commercial food contains close to the same moisture level as a wild cat's prey. Look for meat as the first ingredient and be sure it's not meat by-products, which can include beaks, feathers, claws, and fur. Also, avoid soy, wheat, corn, and any other grains or nonmeat products. Try not to buy food that has such preservatives as butylated hydroxyanisole (BHA), butylated hydroxytoluene (BHT), propyl gallate, propylene glycol, and ethoxyquin—all of these are implicated in causing cancer in companion animals. Instead, look for brands preserved with vitamins C and E. If you feed your cat different brands in rotation, you can occasionally serve him one preserved with rosemary extract. But because rosemary extract poses some of the same risks as the herb, use it sparingly.

BODY COMPOSITION OF A WILD MOUSE [†]

Component	Mean %	% Based on Standard Deviation	
		High	Low
Water	65.8	69.6	62.0
Protein	56.4	64.6	48.2
Fat	27.2	35.0	19.4

† Source: Jasmine Thomas, Batsheva Glatt, and Ellen S. Dierenfeld, "Proximate, vitamins A and E, and mineral composition of free-ranging cotton mice (Peromyscus gossypinus) from St. Catherines Island," Georgia Wiley InterScience 7 Jun 2004, Volume 23, Issue 3, Pages 253-261.

A Case for Raw Diets

Protein, fat, fiber, and moisture are the four most important elements in cats' diets, but as you'll see, most commercial foods fall short in these areas despite their advertising claims.

Although a diet that consists mainly of commercially raised feeder mice isn't a good idea, the body composition of a mouse can help determine the appropriate percentages of nutrients to include in a homemade diet. You can also use this information to evaluate any commercial diet.

A 2004 study of wild mice found the following body composition, which turns out to be almost identical to adult laboratory mice. This is what a cat would eat if left to its own devices. Use the table above as a benchmark when purchasing commercial food or creating your own recipes. Because water is also part of fat and protein, the means won't add up to 100 percent. The remainder of a mouse (16.4 percent) consists of fiber and, to a lesser extent, carbohydrates.

Additives to Avoid in Cat Food and Supplements

Read all cat food labels carefully. If you see any of the following ingredients on the label, consider switching to a healthier brand:

- **BHA and BHT:** carcinogens (confirmed in rat studies to cause liver damage)
- **carrageenan:** a food thickener that can cause ulcerative colitis and other stomach problems
- **ethoxyquin:** a rubber preservative and pesticide
- **mannitol, xylitol, and sorbitol:** can cause severe digestive upset and possibly kidney problems
- **potassium sorbate:** can irritate skin and eyes
- **propylene glycol:** can cause Heinz body anemia, a type of damage to red blood cells
- **sodium benzoate:** can adversely affect the central nervous system and cause allergic reactions as well as stomach irritations

Some cats don't seem to make the connection that mice are their natural prey, yet others want to eat nothing else.

Benefits of a Raw-Meat–Based Diet

- loads of energy

- elimination of stomach problems, such as diarrhea, vomiting, and constipation

- shiny coat

- improved muscle tone

- smaller, nearly odorless stool

- clean, sparkling white teeth

- nice, clean breath

- a decrease in itching and allergy problems

- maintenance of ideal urinary pH (6 to 6.5)

- a strong immune system, leading to better resistance to infections

- a lot less shedding, with rare hairball sightings

Cats Need a High-Protein Diet

Protein, made up of one or more amino acid chains, is the backbone of all growth and tissue repair in animals. Cats require not only a large percentage of protein in their diets for building and maintaining their bodies, protein is also their primary source of energy. Because cats usually excrete excess protein in urine, too much protein usually isn't a problem unless a cat has advanced or end-stage renal failure. If fed too little protein, however, cats will literally waste away as their bodies begin to break down the protein in their own muscles. Mice and other meats contain the correct amount of protein, whereas most commercial foods, whether canned or dry, contain less than optimal amounts of protein.

All protein is not created equal, and to maintain optimal health, cats need a wide variety of amino acids in their diet. Feathers, hair, and other meat by-products traditionally found in prey contain protein but have very little nutritional value to a cat beyond providing some basic fiber. Similarly, the protein in grains such as corn and other nonmeat sources such as soy lack the essential amino acids cats require. The most digestible and bioavailable protein for cats consists of real meat from animal muscle, tissue, and organs.

Dry food seems to contain high levels of protein and, at first glance, appears to have more than canned food. However, to make an apple-to-apple comparison, you need to take into account the moisture percentage of wet food. Then it becomes clear that most canned foods actually have more protein on a dry matter basis than dry food.

Cats Need Fat

Cats' livers metabolize dietary fat for energy, and what the cat's body doesn't use it either stores or excretes through bile. Unlike humans, cats don't suffer from cholesterol problems and require a fairly high amount of fat in their diets. As with proteins, all fats don't have the same component structure.

Unfortunately, scientists don't know the optimal ratio of omega-6 to omega-3 fatty acids in a cat's diet. We do know that cats require fat in their diets in the form of unsaturated fatty acids—arachidonic acid (AA), docosahexaenoic acid (DHA), and eicosapentaenoic acid (EPA) from fish, poultry, and other meats—because these fatty acids are essential for cats' metabolism and also help maintain their beautiful coats.

Adding flax seed oil or hemp seed oil isn't going to satisfy the omega-3 requirement in a cat's diet because cats have a very limited ability to convert alpha-linolenic into EPA and DHA. To that end, cats must get omega-3 fatty acids from animal rather than plant sources. Grass-fed animals are higher in omega-3 fatty acids than grain-fed animals, and cold-water fish such as wild salmon, sardines, mackerel, trout, and eel provide good amounts of DHA and EPA. Because dry food consists mainly of carbohydrates, it lacks the vital nutrients—including the fats—cats need to stay healthy.

Dry Food Contains Excess Carbohydrates

Unlike humans, cats have little or no nutritional need for carbohydrates and instead use protein and fat as energy sources. Animal tissue is very low in carbohydrates, and the small amounts of predigested grains, vegetables, berries, nuts, and seeds in the stomach of a cat's prey are more than enough to satisfy a cat's extremely limited carbohydrate needs. Grains frequently cause allergy problems and intestinal upset in cats, so avoid giving them altogether if you can.

Unfortunately, dry food has a high carbohydrate percentage—30 percent and above in most cases, which is almost six times greater than a cat needs! It's a pity carbohydrate percentages aren't listed on most commercial canned and dry food brands. You can calculate the dry matter percentages of fat and fiber in commercial food using the same method that allows you to determine the percentage of protein. To figure out the carbohydrate content, add up the dry matter percentages of fat, fiber, and protein and subtract this number from one hundred.

Comparing Protein Percentages in Dry versus Canned Food

A quick way to determine the true protein content of any food is to divide the protein percentage listed on the cat food label by the percent of the food that isn't water—that is, the reciprocal of the moisture percentage as listed on the container. For example, a dry food with 20 percent protein and 10 percent moisture content has a 90 percent dry content, and 20 divided by 90 is 0.2222, or 22.22 percent protein.

Compare this with a brand of wet food that contains 10 percent protein and 80 percent moisture. In this case, the dry portion is only 20 percent of the total content (1.00 minus 0.80), making the protein percentage 10 divided by 20, or 50 percent—more than twice the protein of the dry food. Cats require 40 to 50 percent protein on a dry matter basis, giving another strong reason to use canned over dry food.

An easy rule-of-thumb is that dry food contains four times the amount of an equivalent ingredient in canned cat food. So to compare numbers for protein or any other nutrients between dry and canned food, multiply the canned food number times four.

Should Cats Eat Soy?

Soy is often added to cat food under the guise of protein. This cheap switch in dietary protein makes for a very dangerous ingredient. Feeding soy is not just misguided, it can cause some rather serious problems in cats. Soy causes the following effects:

- It disrupts endocrine function and increases thyroxine (T4) levels in cats. An elevated T4 level can indicate hyperthyroidism.

- It can cause digestive upset, including flatulence.

- By interfering with protein digestion, trypsin inhibitors have caused stunted growth and pancreatic problems in test animals.

- Phytic acids contained in soy inhibit the body's absorption of calcium and other minerals.

- We don't know how the phytoestrogens in soy affect cats but, given that soy isn't a natural part of a cat's diet, it's more likely to have a negative than a positive effect.

A Cat's Ideal Diet

A cat's ideal diet should come almost exclusively from animal sources, with minimal plant material and no grains. This will give your cat the right mix to build and preserve lean muscle mass—a high-moisture, low-carbohydrate, high-protein diet with small amounts of non-bulk–forming fiber and moderate amounts of fat from animal sources. A diet low in carbohydrates and high in meat also promotes somewhat dilute urine while also keeping urinary pH slightly acidic, thus keeping crystals, stones, and other urinary problems at bay. Cats on this balanced, species-appropriate diet run far less risk of being overweight or suffering from digestive upset. You can then add supplements based on your cat's specific health care needs.

Cats use fat and protein, not carbohydrates, for energy. To that end, they need about 25 to 30 percent fat in their diet. Cats need no more than 10 percent carbohydrate content in their diets, with

preferably only 5 to 6 percent carbohydrates. Cats don't have any amylase (the enzyme that helps digest grains and other carbohydrates) in their saliva and have very low levels of amylase in their stomach and pancreas. They aren't built by nature to consume large or even moderate amounts of carbohydrates. They're the ultimate low-carbohydrate species, and excess carbohydrates can cause bloating, obesity, and other health problems. The remainder of a cat's diet should consist of high-quality protein in the form of real meat, including as much of the entire animal as possible.

Cats can't convert beta-carotene into vitamin A, although they can use beta-carotene from pumpkin and other vegetable sources. Also, cats can't produce taurine, so they need it in either a supplement or meat. Because taurine amounts vary so much among different meats and parts of meat, you might want to supplement your cat's diet with taurine.

Natural Food Costs Less

It's less expensive to feed your cats a raw diet rather than a dry or canned diet, because your cats will actually eat less. The following table lists the amount of dry, canned, and raw food your cat needs each day for optimal nutrition.

TYPE OF FOOD	AMOUNT FED PER DAY
Dry (premium)	3/4 cup (48 g) or approximately 4 oz (115 g)
Canned	10 to 11 oz (280 to 308 g)
Raw	1/4 lb equals 4 oz (115 g)

Can Cats Be Vegetarians?

- Although debate exists over whether humans are meant to eat meat, researchers don't dispute that cats are obligate carnivores. Cats simply can't live without meat and the highly bioavailable protein and amino acids (taurine, arginine, methionine, and cysteine, to mention just a few) they contain, as well as certain fatty acids and vitamins found only in animal tissue.

- Cats can develop serious health problems if they eat only a plant- and grain-based diet, even with supplementation. Out of respect for cats, we must recognize the difference in physiology between cats and humans. There are products out there for vegan and vegetarian cats, but if you look at the ingredient listings carefully, you'll notice they contain nonmeat protein sources, nonanimal omega-3 sources, and a lot of vegetables and grains. This kind of food has very little nutritional value for cats. Sadly, diets like these can cause major health problems, including dangerous deficiencies of key amino acids, fatty acids, and vitamins.

Cooking for Your Cat

If you don't feel comfortable feeding your cat raw meat, you can lightly fry it on the outside, leaving the inside raw. Prepare your raw mix as usual. Then, just before serving it, add a little ghee, butter, or olive oil and heat the meat for just a few seconds. If the meat mix seems a bit dry, you can add meat broth or water while warming up the meat to release the meat's aroma.

Your cat will actually have an easier time digesting raw meat than cooked meat because of the enzymes raw meat naturally contains. It's also not easy to determine the nutrients lost in the cooking process, so you'll have more of a challenge adequately supplementing a cooked meat diet. If you choose to cook meat, add digestive enzymes and twice as much taurine as a recipe calls for because cooking decreases enzyme activity in meat. You'll also need to supplement with a feline multivitamin.

Unless your cat has an inflammatory condition, you can include chicken or turkey skin in your raw food mix because it's high in omega-6 fatty acids.

Selecting Meat Protein

A cat's optimal diet should consist of small animals and birds similar to what they might eat if they had to hunt for their food themselves, such as Cornish game hen, guinea fowl, rabbit, quail, mice, vole, gopher, and pheasant. Because these meats aren't always easy to come by, you can instead buy the following from farms or the grocery store: Cornish game hen, turkey, buffalo, bison, ostrich, venison, emu, lamb, elk, and chicken. Meats too high in fat aren't always palatable to cats. Also, some cats have trouble digesting beef, lamb, duck, goose, and pork. Don't form the foundation of your cats' diet on these meats, but most cats don't have a problem with these meats if they eat them occasionally. Fish is high in iodine, and has a high histamine content, but contains beneficial omega-3 fatty acids, so one fish meal a week makes a nice addition to a cat's diet. A good choice is wild salmon, which you can lightly steam before feeding.

Ideally, feed your cats the same quality food that you eat your-self. Try to choose organic vegetables, meats, poultry, and fish. This is

If you don't have the time to cook at each meal, you can make up a large batch of cooked food and freeze it. You can do this by baking a fryer in the oven or pressure-cooking meat to the point where you can run the bones, meat, and cooking water through a heavy-duty blender or grinder (either electric or manual). At mealtime, add a little warm water, then mix and serve. You can also add enzymes, taurine, or any other supplements, such as vitamins and minerals.

particularly important for animal liver; look for organic liver from grass-fed animals, even if you don't feed your cat organic meat of any other kind.

Which Vegetables to Feed?

Feed your cat the vegetables listed in this section in rotation. When making your cat food recipe, use a total of two tablespoons (28 g) of vegetables per pound of meat. Watch carefully for digestive upset, in which case you can safely omit any of these vegetables. Some cats with IBD not only have problems with grains, but also with some vegetables. To avoid this problem, introduce only one vegetable at a time in the diet, and in small amounts.

Finely chop all vegetables to break down the cell walls because cats typically eat predigested vegetable matter in a prey's stomach. If you leave the vegetables in large pieces, your cat won't digest them, and you'll see bits of vegetable in your cat's stools. An excellent option is to use the pulp left over from juicing vegetables in a juicer or to grind vegetables in a food processor. If you use a meat grinder, you can feed vegetables through the chute as is; they'll get finely ground in with the meat.

Did You Know?

Cats shouldn't eat onions or broth containing onions or onion powder. Onions can cause serious damage to red blood cells. If your cat eats onions or something containing onions, be alert for signs such as weakness, lethargy, panting, and weight loss.

Vegetable	Reason for Feeding and Preparation Tips
Carrots	Contain beta-carotene but high in sugar and carbohydrates
Pumpkins	Have a low glycemic load (GL), despite being high on glycemic index (GI) High in fiber, which helps with constipation Taste good to cats, especially canned pumpkin High beta-carotene
Sweet potatoes	Have low glycemic index (GI) High in fiber and beta-carotene

Winter squash
  acorn
  butternut
	High in moisture and fiber, both of which help with constipation; steam to soften the skin and break down cell walls

Summer squash zucchini	High moisture content Mild taste
Celery	Mild diuretic properties Benefits the liver Stimulates appetite Helps relieve digestive upset
Parsnips	High in potassium and fiber
Peas Green beans	Both have mild smell and taste, and contain both soluble and insoluble fiber; both must be cooked to reduce phytic acid, maximizing mineral absorption
Mushrooms	All mushrooms are high in fiber; cooking increases fiber levels and prebiotic amounts
Portabella	High in oligosaccharides, which help feed gut bacteria, and beta-glucans, which boost immune system and have antitumor properties
Maitake and Shiitake	High in beta-glucans
White buttons	High in fructo-oligosaccharides (FOS), a prebiotic

Greens
  dandelion greens
  collard greens
  kale
  Swiss chard
	All contain fiber, beta-carotene, calcium, potassium, and vitamin K; dandelion has kidney-protective benefits

Grasses
  Wheat
  Rye
  Oat
  Barley
	High in vitamins A, B, C, E, and K as well as trace minerals
	High in chlorophyll and anti-oxidants such as Superoxide Dismutase
	
	Reputed to have anti-cancer properties

Vegetables to Avoid

- **onions: cause Heinz body anemia, a type of damage to red blood cells**

- **shallots and leeks: closely related to onions, with similar effects**

- **garlic: may cause Heinz body anemia**

- **vegetables in the nightshade family (white, red, or Yukon gold potatoes; tomatoes; bell peppers; and eggplant); solanine can cause digestive problems**

- **iceberg lettuce: has very little nutritional value; instead, use fresh wheat grass on the side or mixed in food**

- **raw alfalfa and red clover: contain coumarin, an anticoagulant**

- **radishes: are difficult to digest; can cause gas and bloating**

Fiber

Fiber is the portion of plants not digested by enzymes in the intestinal tract. It's classified as either soluble or insoluble. Soluble fiber partially dissolves in water and forms a gel; insoluble fiber doesn't. Soluble fiber delays the time it takes for food to make its way through the intestine. Many foods contain a combination of soluble and insoluble fiber. Examples of soluble fiber include psyllium husk, oats, and beet pulp. Although many vegetables contain both types of fiber, artichokes, Brussels sprouts, and mushrooms are higher in soluble fiber than insoluble fiber.

Insoluble fiber, on the other hand, draws water into the colon, speeds up intestinal transit time, and results in a softer and larger stool. Wheat bran, which can irritate some cats' digestive systems, contains insoluble fiber. Carrots, pumpkins, zucchini, sweet potatoes, spinach, and celery contain more insoluble than soluble fiber. Although fiber might benefit some cats with diarrhea, constipation, and more generally IBD, healthy cats don't need bulking agents in their diets. However, some scientific evidence shows soluble fiber's binding action slows down the body's glucose absorption, stabilizing blood glucose levels. Moderation is the key, even when fiber might be medically warranted, such as for diabetic cats.

Cats don't need a lot of fiber, especially the bulk-forming kind, but some fiber such as the types shown here can help your cat's intestinal health. (Above: carrots, celery, zucchini, mushrooms, and peas)

Vegetables to Use Occasionally

- asparagus: helps build blood and helps the digestive tract; can irritate kidneys, so don't use if your cat has a urinary problem or flare-up

- spinach: although it is high in fiber and moisture, its high oxalic acid content can bind with calcium in food and block calcium absorption

- cruciferous vegetables (broccoli, Brussels sprouts, cabbage, cauliflower, kohlrabi, and turnips): can be difficult to digest and cause bloating and gas (adding ground roasted caraway seeds to the mix alleviates this problem); contain goitrogens, which can interfere with the actions of the thyroid gland, especially if fed raw

- beets: benefit various health conditions but because of its detoxifying action, introduce them slowly

What About Eggs?

Don't feed your cats raw egg whites because they contain avidin, which binds to the B-vitamin biotin contained in yolks. When fed together, the avidin binds with all the biotin, preventing your cats' bodies from absorbing the biotin.

Instead, you can feed your cats raw egg yolks alone or in conjunction with lightly poached egg whites because cooking deactivates avidin, taking care of the imbalance issue. If you feed your cats eggs only occasionally, you can feed them the whole egg, including the shell, by running it through the grinder. However, if you plan to include eggs in your regular recipe, plan on lightly cooking the egg whites but leaving the yolks raw.

In addition to the tools shown here–cleaver, kitchen shears, gloves, food chopper, cutting board, bowl, and storage containers–you will need a large bowl to hold the ground mix, and possibly one or more large cutting boards for making your own raw food.

Invest in a high-quality, sharp cleaver. Chinese supermarkets are a wonderful, inexpensive source for these. Most cleavers are so sharp that one strong whack is all you need to sever a chicken joint. Sharp kitchen shears and small carpenter's hatchets also come in handy for cutting up necks into smaller pieces.

Happy Cat Grocery Checklist

Meat (the smaller the animal or bird, the better)

bison

chicken

Cornish game hen

deer

elk

emu

goat

guinea fowl

lamb

mice, vole, gopher, and other rodents

quail, pheasant, and other smalls birds

rabbit

turkey

Vegetables

carrots

celery

cruciferous vegetables

broccoli

Brussels sprouts

cabbage

cauliflower

kohlrabi

turnips

green beans

grasses and greens

collard greens

dandelion greens

kale

Swiss chard

Rye, oat, barley and wheat

peas

pumpkin

summer squash

zucchini

sweet potatoes

winter squash

acorn

butternut

Oils

chicken skins

wild salmon or other fish body oil

pork lard

trimmed beef fat

Supplements

calcium source, such as bone meal or eggshell, calcium carbonate, or calcium lactate powder

taurine powder or capsules

Safety Concerns

Because both salmonella and Escherichia coli (E. coli) can lead to food poisoning, use care when handling raw meat, and follow proper thawing techniques. Barring mishandling, neither salmonella nor E. coli typically cause problems for cats. This is because a carnivore's intestinal tract is about a third the length of a human's, which means meat enters and exits their digestive systems in about twelve hours. Their strong digestive juices, which have a high percentage of hydrochloric acid, quickly get to work digesting the meat, before it can putrefy in the intestinal tract. If you're nervous about either bacteria or parasites developing, consider freezing the food, defrosting, and rinsing it before use. Freezing kills any parasites that may exist in meat and inactivates microbes until the meat thaws.

Happy Cat Kitchen Supply Kit Checklist

cutting boards

disposable gloves

food grinder or processor

large glass or ceramic mixing bowls

large plastic shopping bags

meat cleaver

sturdy utensil, such as a serving spoon

vinegar for cleanup

OPTIONAL HAPPY CAT FOOD SUPPLIES

cod liver oil or vitamins **A** and **D**

vitamin **B, C,** and **E**

minerals

trace minerals or seaweeds, such as dulse and kelp

cold-pressed grape seed oil or extra virgin olive oil

gelatin

tablets containing kidneys, thymus, spleen, and other glands, often available as multiglandular formulations

Can Cats Eat Raw Bones?

Cats can eat raw bones, as long as the bones are soft and manageable. Barring small kittens, most cats can handle raw bones quite well because they're naturally equipped to do so. Don't chop poultry necks into very small pieces because that poses a choking hazard. However, if the neck segments are too large, they might intimidate a cat and he might lose interest in eating them. So keep the pieces just large enough for your cat to get some benefit from chewing them but not so small that they might choke him.

The easiest bones for a cat to eat are Cornish game hen necks followed by chicken necks. Duck and turkey necks are another excellent choice because they have a good deal of meat, and cats can spend a lot of time chewing and gnawing on them, even dislodging existing tartar. Start by serving your cat necks; then you can move on to whole quail, whole mice, and whole small birds. Once your cat grows more comfortable eating smaller bones, you can transition to larger, bone-in meats, such as chicken backs and wings.

Because meat cuts with a high bone ratio can lead to an imbalance in the diet, cats should ideally eat small prey, such as quail or game hen, in their entirety. Most cats can polish one of these off in one to three sittings, making them ideal for your cats. Not only is the calcium-phosphorous level balanced, but cats also get the benefit of chewing on bones. This helps keep their teeth clean and plaque-free.

Never feed cats cooked bones because cooking causes bones to become brittle, making them more likely to splinter and cause internal bleeding as well as intestinal blockage. Supervise all meals involving bones, because occasionally a tooth can get stuck in a neck segment or meat can get caught between a cat's teeth. If this occurs, gently pry the meat or neck segment loose and give it to your cat again. Most cats can handle small, soft bones just fine, but it's always good to keep a watchful eye. Very large or hard bones, such as beef or deer bones, can cause problems such as cracked teeth.

Unlike humans and certain other species, cats have very specific dietary requirements. So keep it simple, and follow a few basic rules:

- If you feed your cat as close to a whole animal or bird as possible, he'll get the correct ratio of meat, organs, and bone, protein, moisture, fat, fiber, and carbohydrate percentages will fall into place.

- If you can't feed whole birds and animals, then replicate the percentage of nutrients contained in mice and aim to provide between 1.2 and 1.4 times as much calcium as phosphorus in your cat's diet.

- Use herbs and nutritional supplements sparingly. A significant number of the herbs and supplements that are good for humans aren't safe for cats.

- Make sure any supplements you use come from animal sources, such as omega-3 from fish oil, not flax, coconut, grape seed, or hemp seed oil.

- Keep vegetables down to 10 percent or less of the overall diet, depending on how well your cat handles them.

- Avoid grains and cow's milk.

- Make sure your cat's diet includes preformed vitamin A because cats can't convert beta-carotene into vitamin A.

- Make sure your cat's diet includes preformed niacin (B3) (meat, particularly chicken breast, contains a healthy amount of niacin) because cats can't convert tryptophan into niacin.

- Give your cat enough of the amino acids taurine and arginine, both found in meat; provide a taurine supplement, or feed extra hearts, because cats' bodies absorb only a small percentage of their taurine intake.

You can make eggshell powder inexpensively at home. Rinse out empty eggshells and keep them in a container until you have several. Place the eggshells on a cookie sheet and bake at 300°F (149°C) for 10 minutes. Baking dries out the eggshells, making them easier to grind; it also kills off any lingering bacteria and traces of any coating. Remove the eggshells from the oven and grind them to a fine powder in a coffee grinder dedicated to this use. One large, ground eggshell contains 1,800 to 2,200 milligrams of usable calcium and 75 to 80 milligrams of phosphorus.

If you follow these basic concepts of good nutrition, you'll avoid many of the common ailments cats are predisposed to. But change takes time. At a minimum, select high-quality kibble and canned food high in human-grade meat and low in grains. Ideally, feed your cat a raw-food diet. Work slowly toward this goal and at a comfortable pace for you and your cat. As you incorporate elements of the raw diet into your cat's lifestyle and make the transition, you'll notice a healthier cat with a happier disposition.

CHAPTER THREE

Raw Diet Recipes

"Dogs eat. Cats dine."

ANNE TAYLOR

Transitioning your cat to a raw diet is an important step in achieving total wellness for your cat. The goal is to eventually have your cat on an entirely raw diet, be it small birds and animals or ground meat. This chapter guides you through that process, beginning with suggestions for how to incorporate raw foods into your cat's existing diet and moving on to step-by-step instructions for preparing raw meals. Your cat should transition completely within two to three months. Be patient, and use bribery if necessary; the rewards will be well worth it.

An adult cats needs to eat approximately 20 calories per pound (455 g) of body weight, which is equal to 4 tablespoons, or 1/4 cup (55 g) of food.

Prepackaged Raw Meat

If preparing raw food for your cat isn't feasible, you can order meat from various independent meat farmers or purchase commercial, premade mixes. Most of these manufacturers sell raw foods that have a mix of ground meat, organs, and bone, with or without vegetables. You can usually find them in the freezer section of specialty pet stores. Some of these come in patty form, others, as small, single-serving–sized medallions. These mixes are more expensive than home-prepared food, but the convenience factor is a big plus. Several are less expensive than quality canned food. You can also use them in the transition phase if needed.

Transitioning to a Raw Diet

Some cats do just fine switching to an all-raw diet in one or two meals. But for others, sudden changes in diet can lead to digestive upset. Listen to what your cat is trying to tell you to determine the best transition strategy.

In most cases, without the strong smell of commercial food, cats don't seem to recognize real meat as food. In such situations, hiding the raw meat in canned food offers the path of least resistance.

If your cat dislikes the texture of canned food, skip the switch from dry to canned food. Instead try these out with powdered eggshell powder:

- chopped liver

- finely chopped gizzards

- chunked muscle meat, cooked or raw

If you currently feed your cat dry food and she absolutely refuses to eat meat, one way to transition her to a raw diet is to first get her used to the texture of commercial wet food.

First, prepare some cat food using the Mix-and-Match Recipe

Some cats like bone-less breast meat cut up into chunks. You can even very lightly cook the outside of the meat, leaving it pink inside. This releases the aroma of the meat and gets your cat interested in it. Later, you can add some of these cooked meat chunks into your cat's canned food so it becomes something of a treasure hunt for him.

Matrix on page 79, leaving out only the vegetables.

1. Mix 1/4 teaspoon (1.2 g) of the raw meat mix into your cat's commercial food so she can't distinguish the raw meat from her usual wet food. Decrease the amount of commercial food by 1/4 teaspoon (1.2 g) to keep the amount you feed her the same as before.

2. Increase the amount of ground raw meat mix by 1/4 teaspoon (1.2 g) each day while simultaneously adjusting the amount of wet commercial food.

3. By now your cat should be eating all raw food. Feed 2 table-spoons (28 g) of 100 percent raw meat mix per meal.

4. Instead of 100 percent raw meat mix, prepare the recipe with vegetables included. Cats usually readily accept canned pump-kin, so that's a good vegetable to try first in your recipe.

5. Feed your cat the complete recipe of 2 tablespoons (28 g) per meal; if she doesn't accept the meat mixed with vegetables, sprinkle a condiment on top of the mix.

Sprinkle as many bribe foods as necessary and vary the meat or vegetables in your mix until your cat is eating 100 percent raw food. Be prepared for the complete transition (steps 1 through 5) to take as long as one to three months, if not longer. During this time, never let your cat go more than a day without food because cats, particularly obese ones, can develop a serious health problem known as fatty liver disease.

Kitty Condiments

Limit these to no more than 5 percent of your cat's overall food intake, and try not to feed these long-term. If your cat won't accept a homemade raw diet without bribery, rotate the bribe foods to minimize any possible negative effects of feeding one of these foods over a long period of time.

- hard Italian cheese, such as parmesan, asiago, pecorino, or Romano
- nutritional or brewer's yeast
- real bacon bits
- unsalted butter
- clarified butter, also known as ghee
- extra virgin olive oil
- dried meat liver, crumbled or cut up into small pieces
- fresh-sliced or pureed raw liver
- cooked chicken or turkey breast cut up into small chunks
- bonito fish flakes
- dried seaweed sheets or dulse flakes
- crushed commercial cat treats
- ground beef dust powder
- nitrate-free, minimally processed deli meat, such as turkey or ham
- baby food meat, such as Gerber and Beechnut (without onion powder or broth because onions can cause anemia in cats)
- water from canned salmon or tuna, but not the tuna itself, which can lead to a vitamin E deficiency and cause a serious skin disease known as steatitis
- anything that your cat considers a treat, even unlikely vegetables and fruits such as avocado, cantaloupe, or watermelon

Nutritional Supplements and Vitamins

Although meat contains taurine, vitamins, essential fatty acids, minerals, and other requirements for a healthy cat, there's good reason to supplement even homemade cat food because meats vary in nutrient amounts, and store-bought meat is never as fresh as freshly caught prey.

Required Supplements

Several organizations publish nutritional requirements for cats. You can get this information for free on the Internet at the organizations' official websites. See the Resources section for specific organizations.

You can toss all supplements in the grinder along with the meat and veggies. If the vitamins come in soft gel tabs, such as vitamins A and E, pierce it with a thumbtack and squirt it into the mix. Or you can add the vitamins to each meal at feeding time.

If using ground meat without bones, you must provide your cat with calcium supplementation. Other than that, taurine is the only other critical supplement. If you plan on freezing the ground mix, you can supplement vitamins A, E, and B-complex to make up for loss from the freezing process.

These don't have to be special "pet" or "cat" supplements. In general, powders or pills are best, and capsules are better than tablets because tablets contain more fillers. You can use human-grade supplements without added flavorings and additives.

Taurine, an amino acid available in both powder and tablet form, is critical for healthy eyes, normal heart function, and the absorption of dietary fats. Many scientific studies have demonstrated that taurine helps with epilepsy, diabetes, and liver and heart problems in cats, to name just a few disorders.

If cats don't get enough taurine in their diet, they may become blind and develop serious heart problems. Because cats aren't very efficient at producing taurine, they get this extremely important amino acid in only two ways—from meat and in the form of a supplement.

Although meat contains taurine, levels vary greatly across different meat sources and even within parts of the same animal. For instance, pork contains more taurine than chicken, and chicken legs contain more taurine than other parts of chicken, such as breast meat. Processing, in particular cooking, leads to significant loss in taurine levels—as much as 60 percent with baking and 80 percent with boiling.

Also, the composition of foods in a cat's diet has a direct impact on taurine loss. Several studies prove that adding rice bran to cat food leads to greater taurine depletion, with similar results for soy. Cats that eat dry food also lose more taurine in their stool.

Because cats don't eat rice bran, kibble, and soy protein in the wild, it stands to reason that a diet composed of cats' natural prey would lead to the lowest taurine depletion. However, even when cats eat a raw-meat-based diet, normal digestive processes still degrade taurine production. Because excess taurine won't harm your cats, it's better to err on the side of giving at least 250 mg of taurine per day to each of your cats. If you cook the meat in your cat's diet, you'll need to compensate even more for taurine loss by giving 500 mg daily.

Key Daily Vitamin Supplements for Average-Size Cats:

- **vitamin A: 500 international units (IU)**
- **vitamin B-complex: 10 mg or 2.5–3 ml**
- **vitamin E: 200 IU**
- **vitamin C: 250 mg in calcium ascorbate form at times of stress**
- **vitamin D: 50 IU**

When selecting a brand of multivitamin capsules marketed for cats, check the label to make sure the capsules will meet the daily requirements for cats. Also, look for a brand that has the fewest possible additives and fillers.

OPTIONAL SUPPLEMENTS

Aim to feed a one-month-old kitten a total of one to two teaspoons (5–10 g) of raw food daily, increasing in two-week increments to three to four tablespoons (42–55 g) a day as your kitten approaches adulthood.

You may need to give your cat optional supplements if you feed only two to three types of meat on a routine basis or start with the boneless meat recipe in this chapter. Our understanding about cat nutrition is evolving, and because a cat's system is so different from any other animal's, it's never a good idea simply to extrapolate information from what we know about humans or dogs. The following supplements are optional:

- lecithin granules from egg yolks (during hairball season): contents of one size 0 capsule, which typically contains 500 mg per pound (455 g) of food

- trace minerals: $1/2$ teaspoon (2.5 g) for every 3.5 to 4 pounds (1.6 to 1.8 kg) of meat mix

or

- sea vegetables, such as dulse, kelp, Irish moss, and algae: one teaspoon (5 g) in powdered form for every 4 pounds (1.8 kg) of food

Use sea vegetables cautiously because their high iodine content can overstimulate the thyroid gland, and some believe cats are rather prone to hyperthyroidism. Also, because bones contain trace minerals, add either trace mineral drops or sea vegetables only if you aren't feeding bones to your cat in any form.

Cats with health issues can also benefit from supplements and diet modifications. For more information, see the Diets for Specific Health Conditions on page 83.

How to Prepare Raw Cat Food at Home

With the exception of whole prey, you can prepare the recipes in this chapter once every four to six weeks, store them in the freezer, and feed them to your cat each day, just as you would commercial wet food. Despite what you might think, fresh, raw meat doesn't smell unpleasant.

> Pique your cat's curiosity and increase her enjoyment of food by adding some warm water to it at serving time. Warm water will help if your mix is too gooey, and it will also bring out the aroma of the meat, which will please your cat.

A freshly used meat grinder sitting on the counter is just begging for inspection.

Meat Grinders

Investing in a high-quality meat grinder will make cooking meals at home much easier. You'll need one sturdy enough to grind bones, although most meat grinders don't advertise the fact that you can use them for this purpose. Some manufacturers might even consider a warranty voided if their grinders were used for this purpose. The grinders mentioned in the Resources section at the back of the book have been used to grind such animals as rabbits, game hens, turkeys, and chickens. Of these, turkey bones present the greatest challenge, but mashing them with a hammer or rubber mallet beforehand softens them up enough to go through most meat grinders. If this doesn't work, you can also try cutting the larger bones lengthwise. We use chicken in this book because it's readily available, but any small animal or bird should go through a heavy-duty meat grinder.

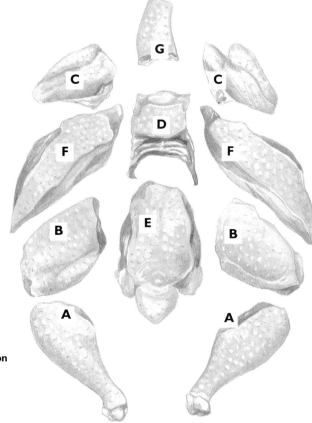

A. legs
B. thighs
C. wings
D. part of back portion
E. tail end of back portion
F. breasts
G. neck

Whole Ground Chicken Meat Mix

This recipe should provide enough for six weeks' worth of food for two cats of average weight and size.

■ INGREDIENTS

4 whole young chicken fryers (not roaster, which are older) approximately 4 pounds (1.8 kg) each, with skin

Giblets and organs that come with the four fryers—liver, kidneys, heart, and gizzards, but not the neck (save this for cats to chew on while you grind the chickens)

1 pound (455 g) vegetables* choose from the table on page 54.

4 eggs, no shell—just the yolks and cooked whites

13,500 mg L-Taurine or 5 teaspoons (25 g) taurine powder: for most brands, $^1/_4$ teaspoon (1.2 g) of taurine powder equals 675 mg or add 1 pound (455 g) of hearts

32 ounces or 4 cups (950 ml) of either spring water or homemade chicken broth (See recipe to follow.)

25,000 IU vitamin A

2,500 IU vitamin D

or

cod liver oil in place of vitamins A and D: as many soft gels as needed to get to 8,500 to 10,00 IU of vitamin D in the brand you use

vitamin E: 9,000 IU (because of the addition of fish oil and to compensate for vitamin E lost in the freezing process)

500 mg vitamin B-complex

10,000 mg wild salmon oil

optional ingredients: $^1/_2$ teaspoon (2.5 ml) trace mineral drops or 1 teaspoon (5 g) of sea vegetables and $^1/_4$ teaspoon (1.2 g) egg yolk lecithin

*Depending on the water content of the veggies, this can be as little as one cup or as high as two cups in volume. Fresh, in-season, organic vegetables are ideal, but you can use frozen ones. In fact, you don't even need to thaw frozen vegetables to grind them. For pumpkin, you can use canned pumpkin. But make sure you use pure canned pumpkin, not pumpkin-pie filling. If using grams rather than cups, use 45 g in place of one cup and 90 g in place of two cups. While these amounts are not exact conversions, they keep the vegetable between 5 to 10 percent of the overall recipe.

1. Line your entire counter top with large plastic shopping bags, overlapping at the seams to prevent juice from dripping onto the counter. If you wish, you can also line your sink with plastic bags for quicker cleanup.

2. Place large bowls or dishes (to hold cut-up meat) and cutting boards on top of the plastic bags. Assemble the grinder by placing the inner sharp flat side of the cutting blade toward the spout end of the grinder. Start with the disk with the smallest holes so the ground meat will more closely resemble commercial food. Over time, you can move to the disk with larger holes for a more coarsely ground mix.

3. Fill your stockpot with half the broth or water plus canned pumpkin (if you prefer this to fresh veggies). Mix well.

4. Place the stockpot containing broth and any pre-ground vegetables in your sink to hold the ground mix. Then position the grinder sideways so that the grinder spout is directly over this bowl or pot.

5. Cut up a chicken into several pieces (how many depends on the size of your grinder), first at each joint, then in the middle lengthwise or across the back.

6. Feed chicken parts in the grinder chute, alternating with veggies—that is, intersperse liquids and soft ingredients with bony chicken parts to give the grinder a break.

7. Mix all ingredients in the stockpot.

8. Spoon the mix into canning jars, leaving room in each jar at the top for expansion. You can also use disposable plastic containers if you wish. A pint-size container holds about six meals' worth. Each time you use up a jar from the fridge, remove another from the freezer and place in the fridge. In most refrigerators, a container takes between a day to a day and a half to thaw completely. An easy approach is to always have two jars in the fridge—one in current use and the other defrosting.

9. To clean up, fold all the bags over and disinfect the sink and the exterior of the grinder with a spray of hydrogen peroxide followed by vinegar. You can run all the grinder parts through the dishwasher, which should disinfect them.

After the disk and other parts of the grinder are clean and dry, rub them with some edible oil, such as grape seed or olive oil, to keep rust at bay.

Rainy Day Chicken Broth

This clear chicken broth recipe provides fifteen to sixteen cups (3.5 to 3.8 l) of broth. It should take about three to four hours to prepare, largely unattended, so it's a great weekend cooking project. Make a large batch by doubling the amounts in this recipe to use later in other broth-based recipes. You can freeze it in ice-cube trays. At each meal, use a defrosted cube of broth to make your cat's food more palatable. Chicken broth makes the ground raw meat mixture easier to handle by making it less gluelike and gooey. It also makes for a delicious pick-me-up for sick cats. If your cat has lost her appetite or has digestive upset, administer 5 to 10 ml of broth using a plastic syringe. Some cats consider broth a treat and will happily lap it up from a bowl.

■ INGREDIENTS

bones from 2 whole or cut-up chicken fryers or bones from 6 to 8 pounds (2.7 to 3.6 kg) of chicken thighs

1 cup (225 g) finely chopped mushrooms

1/2 teaspoon (2.5 ml) apple cider vinegar or lemon juice

1 medium-sized carrot, chopped into small pieces

2 chopped celery stalks with leaves

1 bunch flat-leaf parsley

16 to 20 cups (3.8 to 4.7 l) of water

■ INSTRUCTIONS

1. Place the chicken bones in a soup pot, leaving plenty of room for adding water.

2. Add in the rest of the ingredients except water.

3. Pour in enough water to cover all the ingredients with an additional couple of inches.

4. Partially cover the pot.

5. Bring the pot to a boil initially, then lower the heat and simmer for three to four hours. During this time, add more water if needed.

6. Skim the foam that comes to the surface during the cooking process.

7. Remove the pot cover for the last few minutes of cooking.

8. Strain the broth through a fine-mesh strainer into a bowl. Let it cool, then cover and refrigerate it.

9. After one or two days in the refrigerator, remove the hardened layer of fat on the broth.

10. Store in the refrigerator for three to five days, or freeze for future use.

To help keep your cat's eating area germ-free, prepare two spray bottles. Fill one with white vinegar and the other with 3 percent hydrogen peroxide (available at most drugstores). Mist your cat's eating area first with one, and then the other; the order doesn't matter. A few spray mists in quick succession will kill bacteria. Make sure you store each of the two ingredients in separate spray bottles because they're less effective if mixed together.
Source: *Science*, 1997

Boneless Raw Meat Recipes

Generally speaking, meat is much higher in phosphorous than calcium, and bones are higher in calcium than phosphorous. When a cat eats the whole animal, Mother Nature takes care of the calcium-phosphorous ratio in a cat's diet, with the meat, organs, and bones providing the ideal mix. Cats' prey animals, such as mice, rabbits, and quail, can have quite a wide range of ratios, ranging from one part calcium for each part phosphorous (a 1:1 ratio) to two and a half times the calcium as phosphorous (a 2.5:1 ratio). The safest option is to keep a cat's dietary calcium-to-phosphorous ration between 1:2 and 1:4. Ground whole chicken with skin provides a 1:4 ratio, which is almost the same as that of an adult mouse. Ground-up chicken backs or breastbones would have too much calcium compared with phosphorous. That's why it's best to stick as close as possible to feeding the animal or bird in its entirety.

If you can't grind meat with bones at home, you can add either calcium or bone meal to boneless meat to provide the ideal calcium-to-phosphorous ratio. Because different meats and veggies have varying amounts of calcium and phosphorus, you must first determine how much calcium and phosphorous a given type of meat contains; then you can calculate how much calcium to add to achieve the ideal calcium to phosphorous ratio. The Mix-and-Match Recipe Matrix (see page 79) has done these calculations to determine the calcium supplementation amount. If you feed your cat a meat other than the ones included in that matrix, you can go to the U.S. Department of Agriculture's website and use their food calculator to get this information (see Online Nutritional Information Resources, right).

Online Nutritional Information Resources

Several online sites, such as the ones listed below, have nutritional information for most meats, including fat percentages, potassium, calcium, and phosphorous amounts:

www.ag.uiuc.edu/~food-lab/nat/mainnat.html

www.nal.usda.gov/fnic/foodcomp/search/

www.nutritiondata.com

Bone Meal or Calcium: Which Source Is Better?

One teaspoon (5 g) of eggshell powder contains 1,800 to 2,200 mg of elemental or usable calcium in carbonate form. This is based on research findings that one large eggshell yielding approximately one teaspoon (5 g) of eggshell powder, ranges from 5,000 to 5,500 mg total calcium, with 39 percent being the usable amount. You may also use calcium lactate powder, but because it contains only 13 percent usable calcium, it will take more teaspoons of calcium lactate powder than of eggshell powder to reach the same usable amount of calcium.

To get 1,000 mg of elemental calcium, you'd need to use one of the following sources of calcium (Note: these sources contain progressively less usable calcium amounts):

> 2,500 mg calcium carbonate
>
> or
>
> 2,778 mg eggshell powder
>
> or
>
> 4,762 mg calcium citrate
>
> or
>
> 7,692 mg calcium lactate
>
> or
>
> 11,111 mg calcium gluconate

If you want to get closer to feeding whole animals and birds, bone meal might be a better choice than eggshell powder because animal and bird bones contain a lot more than just calcium. However, some cats with urinary problems seem to do better with calcium carbonate rather than bone meal. Also, bone meal carries the risk of bovine spongiform encephalopathy and may contain contaminants such as lead and arsenic. If you wish to feed bone meal, some reputable manufacturers make this product. Most brands contain a 2:1 ratio of calcium to phosphorous, so each teaspoon (5 g) contains 1,000 mg of calcium and 500 mg of phosphorous. Thus for each 1,000 mg of calcium your cat receives, she gets about half that amount of phosphorous.

Not-Just-for-Sunday Turkey Dinner

This recipe uses ground turkey muscle meat as well as turkey liver, heart, and gizzards from the grocery store. It should provide enough food for one cat for five or six days.

This recipe rounds the calcium amount to 1,400 mg, the bare minimum you need to add. If you can't find hearts, add an extra 500 mg of taurine. If you change the liver source or use a different meat source, you'll need to make appropriate adjustments. If the phosphorous levels in the replacement meat source aren't higher than turkey muscle, liver, and gizzards, you can add close to the same amount of calcium or eggshell powder.

> **When feeding cooked meat,** add one and a half to twice the taurine that's in a raw diet to compensate for taurine lost. Also reserve nutrient-rich cooking water for later reheating and feeding.

■ INGREDIENTS

1 pound (455 g) raw ground turkey muscle meat (the darker the meat, the higher its taurine content)

1 piece of raw turkey liver (2 ounces, or 55 g)

1 raw heart

3^1/2 ounces (100 g) chicken or turkey gizzards

2 tablespoons (28 g) veggies, very finely minced or pureed in a food processor

1400 mg calcium carbonate powder, 1 teaspoon (5 g) eggshell powder, or 1^1/2 teaspoons (7.5 g) bone meal powder*

1 raw egg yolk

1 lightly cooked egg white

1 teaspoon (5 ml) salmon body oil in liquid form or 500 mg squirted from soft gels

1,000 mg taurine

homemade meat broth or spring water to help with consistency; avoid canned broth because most brands contain onions and in some cases, garlic

2,500 IU vitamin A

250 IU vitamin D

100 mg vitamin B-complex

1000 IU vitamin E

Optional supplements:

1 teaspoon (5 ml) powdered gelatin; because bones contain cartilage, this serves as a proxy

^{1}/4 teaspoon (1.2 g) kelp or dulse to make up for trace minerals usually present in bones

^{1}/8 to ^{1}/4 teaspoon (0.6 to 1.2 g) egg yolk lecithin during hairball season

*Appendix A contains this calculation. You shouldn't need to do any calculations if you use the recipe matrix in this chapter. However, if you create your own recipe, use the Appendix calculations as a guide.

Continued

■ INSTRUCTIONS

1. Puree the vegetables or use veggie pulp from a juicer.

2. Finely chop the raw heart, gizzards, and liver.

3. Mix all ingredients (with your hands if need be) and blend well. You can add more water or broth if the consistency is too gooey and gluelike.

4. Transfer to storage containers and freeze.

5. At feeding time, warm up the food a bit and serve, typically about 2 to 3 tablespoons (28 to 42 g) per average-size cat per meal.

NOTE: When possible, buy larger cuts of meat to grind. Use liver, heart, and gizzard from any animal, if organs of matching animal are unavailable.

Column A +	Column B +	Column C or	Column D or	Column E
Meats* (1 lb, or 0.45 kg) + 1 heart, 1 liver, and 1 gizzard	Veggies** 2 tablespoons (28 g) (choose any or mix-and-match)	Calcium powder (elemental amount)	Eggshell powder	Bone meal powder
Turkey	Broccoli	1,300 mg	3/4 teaspoon (3.7 g)	1 1/4 teaspoon (6.2 g)
Beef (10% fat)	Cauliflower	1,300 mg	3/4 teaspoon (3.7 g)	1 1/4 teaspoon (6.2 g)
Lamb	Celery	1,110 mg	2/3 teaspoon (3 g)	1 1/8 teaspoon (5.6 g)
Emu	Mushrooms	1,350 mg	3/4 teaspoon (3.7 g)	1 1/4 teaspoon (6.2 g)
Deer	Peas	1,356 mg	3/4 teaspoon (3.7 g)	1 1/4 teaspoon (6.2 g)
Chicken	Pumpkin	1,063 mg	2/3 teaspoon (3 g)	1 1/8 teaspoon (5.6 g)
Veal	Spinach	1,300 mg	3/4 teaspoon (3.7 g)	1 1/4 teaspoon (6.2 g)
Elk	Squash	1,140 mg	2/3 teaspoon (3 g)	1 1/8 teaspoon (5.6 g)
Bison	Zucchini	1,801 mg	1 teaspoon (5 g)	1 3/4 teaspoon (8.7 g)
Pork	Greens	1,121 mg	2/3 teaspoon (3 g)	1 1/8 teaspoon (5.6 g)
Ostrich	Carrots	1,767 mg	1 teaspoon (5 g)	1 3/4 teaspoon (8.7 g)

*Choose a meat from Column A. Add two tablespoons of any ground vegetable from Column B, and the amount of calcium specified for your meat choice from Columns C, D, or E. Next, add raw yolk and cooked white from one egg for each pound (0.45 kg) of meat plus supplements in the same amounts as specified on page 67.

**See chapter two for a list of vegetables and their nutrient content to determine the best ones for your cat.

Does Your Cat Love Greens?

Some cats love to nibble on grass and catnip. If you like, you can grind some up in a food grinder or processor and add these fresh greens to their food—either commercial or home-made—to help with hairballs. These ground grasses are a natural source of chlorophyll. Some cats prefer the taste of food with added greens.

The most expensive way to go about giving your cat greens to nibble on is to buy a small pot labeled "cat grass." A cheaper option is to purchase large flats of wheat grass from your local health food store.

You can easily grow your own cat grass—which is nothing but wheat grass—from seeds or it can be purchased in pots.

If you have a green thumb, purchase inexpensive wheat berries from a seed store or bulk food section of a natural foods market and plant a few seeds about 1/2 inch (1.5 cm) deep in a pot containing soil. Place it in a garden window or any sunny area, and water regularly. The seeds will begin to sprout in a week or so, and will be ready for munching. You can keep several pots around and stagger the planting period so your cats always have access to greens. Catnip can also be grown from seeds using the same technique. You might need to cover the soil with chicken wire if your cats dig in the soil in anticipation of the catnip.

If your cat enjoys fresh catnip, place some in a paper towel and dry it out in the oven for a few days. When you want to offer your cat some catnip, crush the dried catnip between your fingers and let her sniff them. She might prefer dried catnip, which has a more potent, concentrated scent. Your can put some catnip in her bed or rub it on her toys and scratching post. You can even crush it and placed on top of her food to stimulate her appetite. The possibilities are endless.

How to Get a Cat Interested in Chewing on Raw, Meaty Bones

Poultry necks are soft and spongy, so the bones in them are easier for cats to chew. They make ideal snacks for cats. The four best choices are necks from Cornish game hen, chicken, turkey, and duck.

Cornish game hen necks are ideal for cats that find larger necks intimidating because of their size. These serve as a good first step because many cats readily accept them. Once they acquire the taste and confidence, many are more open to trying chicken and/or turkey necks. Duck and turkey necks are meatier than chicken or game hen necks, so cats sometimes prefer them. However, they also have a large circumference, making them harder for cats to handle. When feeding turkey necks, it might be best to remove the skin first; you don't have to do this for chicken or game hen.

GENERAL GUIDELINES

First, get your cat used to eating breast meat cut up into very small bite-size chunks. You can increase the size over time to the size of playing dice. After your cat is used to chunks, try mixing just one small neck segment into a plate containing several chunks. If she balks, try the following, and keep the chunks separate from the necks so you don't upset her.

If your cat won't eat a whole neck when first presented with it, don't despair. It might just be too big for her. To help with this problem, cut it into several small pieces, preferably at each segment. Use your judgment when cutting up necks because you want to make the pieces small enough to be more manageable, but you don't want your cat to try to swallow them whole. As your cat gets used to chewing on necks, slowly increase the size of the pieces until they reach a size both you and your cat think is ideal.

In the case of turkey necks, cut each neck into six or seven pieces. This should yield smallish cylindrical neck segments. Next, lay these segments flat on the cutting board, and chop them in half again so they look like semicircles. You can even hit them with a rubber mallet against the flat of your cleaver's blade to make them softer and easier for your cat to handle.

Last but not least, it is important to always supervise your cat's bone chewing.

> **As with humans, lack of interest in certain foods could be due to texture, smell, or taste. If your cat refuses raw food, think critically about which aspect may be causing her to reject it.**

You can smear canned food on the necks, dip them in a liquid your cat likes, or rub a dry powder on them. You might need to try all three for a stubborn cat, but don't give up. Chewing on necks will help prevent tartar buildup and save your cat from undergoing dental cleaning under general anesthesia. The idea with these bribes is to keep your cat from walking away after a brief sniff, and focus her attention on the neck. The smell will entice her to lick or bite into it, and once she digs in she will hopefully keep going until she's chewing on the neck.

You can roll the necks in or rub with one or more of the following, based on your cat's tastes:

- 100 percent crumbled or crushed dried meat liver
- real bacon bits
- crushed catnip
- 100 percent dried salmon
- beef dust powder (some butchers carry it, or you can get a commercial version at many pet supply places or online)

Soak, dip, or even marinate the necks in one of your cat's favorite liquids to infuse the necks with smells from her favorite bribe foods. Choose from the following:

- diluted or water-down canned prescription food, such as Hills AD
- meat baby food
- pureed liver run through a blender
- clam, tuna, or salmon juice
- any liquefied commercial canned food

As a last resort, you can try the immersion-in-hot-water trick. You shouldn't cook bones in any way, including microwaving. However, one way to get your cat interested in necks is to entice her with the aroma, and this method releases the meat smell.

Using a pair of tongs, dip a neck segment in boiling water for a count of one Mississippi and no longer. Take it out immediately. At this point, your cat should be interested in the smell if nothing else. If the neck seems to be too cooked, immediately dunk it in ice or run it under cold water. Immersing the neck in boiling water for one second shouldn't cook the neck on the inside; just lightly cook the meat on the outside. This should leave the bones still soft and chewy, without the risk of splintering that can occur with brittle, cooked bones.

Chewing on raw chicken, game hen, or turkey neck segments helps keep plaque from forming. You can feed these to a cat on a commercial canned diet as well. If your cat will accept it, feeding her an entire quail, mouse, or game hen will give her teeth and jaws a workout and might even eliminate the need for annual teeth cleanings under anesthesia.

Diets for Specific Health Conditions

Because you're in control of the ingredients in a home-prepared diet, you can easily adapt a raw recipe if your cat has a health condition, such as feline lower urinary tract disease, chronic renal failure, diabetes, IBD, cancer, or a heart problem.

Lower Urinary Tract Disease (LUTD)

This is the most common urinary problem affecting cats. While cats are less likely to have bacterial infections, they are at risk of developing alkaline urine. You can use these recommendations as a preventative for healthy cats as well as for cats prone to LUTD.

Stay attuned to your cat's habits as he ages. Constant meowing in a previously quiet cat, for instance, can be a sign of hyperthyroidism, hearing loss, or senility.

- Don't feed your cat fish, or feed it in very small quantities.
- Instead of bone meal, use calcium lactate, calcium carbonate, or eggshell powder to balance phosphorous levels in meat.
- Use winter squash as the vegetable source because, unlike most vegetables, it has an acidic effect on urine.
- If available, feed your cat guinea fowl—a type of wild poultry from Africa that can often be found on small family farms around the world—as a meat source.
- Add gizzards to the raw mix, or let your cats chew on gizzards. As an added benefit, it will give your cat's teeth a workout. Gizzards are high in l-methionine, an amino acid that's a natural urine acidifier, which will help keep your cat's urinary pH within the healthy range (a pH of 6 to 6.5).

Chronic Renal Failure

If you are grinding whole meat or feeding whole prey, switch between adding bone meal and calcium with trace minerals. Using only calcium leaves other vital minerals out of the equation.

Traditionally, treatment for kidney failure involved placing cats on a low-protein diet in the belief that this would place less strain on their kidneys. But low-protein diets can harm any cat, including one with declining kidney function. Recent practice has shown that keeping phosphorous levels in check slows down the progression of kidney failure, but lower protein foods don't help and can, in fact, exacerbate muscle wasting. The challenge is that a cat's natural diet consists of meat, which is naturally high in phosphorous. Here are some ways to get around this problem.

- Feed meats lower in phosphorous, such as chicken and turkey rather than beef.
- Substitute cooked egg whites for a portion of the meat; do this slowly, or your little carnivore will protest.
- Use eggshell powder rather than carbonate powder or bone meal to balance phosphorous levels in meat; the Japanese have successfully used eggshell powder as an oral phosphate binder, so you might want to discuss this with your veterinarian as your cat's disease progresses.
- Add soluble fiber such as cooked peas and cooked mushrooms to satisfy the vegetable portion of the diet.
- Include small amounts of celery, which has a mild diuretic action, to the diet.
- Add fermentable fiber, such as beet pulp or psyllium and cooked pumpkin, to the food to help your cat's body trap and excrete excess nitrogen from stool instead of urine; keep in mind that too much fermentable fiber can lead to gas and abdominal bloating, so introduce it and increase the amount slowly, giving no more than a pinch of psyllium each day, which comes out to about one-eighth teaspoon mixed with two tablespoons of water.

Diabetes

Feeding high-carbohydrate foods causes the pancreas to churn out more insulin. The body digests foods with a low glycemic index (under 55) and glycemic load (less than 10) more slowly. These foods produce a gradual increase in blood sugar and insulin levels, reducing the load on a cat's pancreas. Cats with diabetes do best on a high-protein, low-carbohydrate diet because protein is converted more slowly into glucose than carbohydrates, keeping blood glucose levels stable.

- To keep blood glucose levels in check, never feed a diabetic cat potatoes or grains; in general, you shouldn't give these foods to any cat.
- Choose grasses; leafy, green vegetables; and other nonstarchy veggies low on the glycemic index (55 or less), such as peas, zucchini, broccoli, cauliflower, and celery; don't give carrots, which have a high sugar content.
- If your cat can tolerate it, add soluble fiber such as psyllium husk, which human studies demonstrate binds with blood sugar and reduces the need for insulin; for each $1/8$ teaspoon (0.6 g) of psyllium, add 2 tablespoons (28 g) of water.

Children learn valuable social skills and life lessons from having a cat; they also have a lot to offer a cat. Have them accompany you to the veterinarian's office or participate in the examination process when possible.

Inflammatory Bowel Disease

Although we don't know the cause of IBD at this time, we do know the crucial roles diet and the immune system play. Whether your cat has food allergies or problems with her colon or small intestine, the right diet will help keep her on an even keel. Keep the following in mind if your cat suffers from chronic digestive issues:

- Don't ever give your cat with IBD grains because they can irritate the digestive tract or, at the very least, lead to carbohydrate malabsorption.

- Stick to one protein source at a time; you might need to switch to a "novel" protein, such as venison or duck, from time to time.

- Keep in mind that IBD cats with constipation problems tend to do better with insoluble fiber such as canned pumpkin, whereas cats prone to diarrhea benefit more from psyllium fiber (with lots of water) added to their food.

- You can add supplemental L-glutamine, probiotics (acidophilus), prebiotics (fructo-oligosaccharides), and digestive enzymes to each meal, which will improve your cat's nutrient absorption; you can find these three supplements at health food stores or online at various e-retailers.

Liver Disease

Cats have rather sensitive livers, which drugs and chemicals can damage. They're also prone to several rather serious liver diseases, most commonly cholangiohepatitis, which is an inflammation of the liver and bile duct, and fatty liver disease known as hepatic lipidosis.

A cat with liver problems can benefit from additional taurine and celery because animal studies have shown that they increase bile secretion. Avoid fish of any sort in your cat's food. If your cat has cholangiohepatitis, feed her frequent, small meals of extremely bioavailable protein, such as mice and rabbit. If you can't do this, feed her the best organic meat you can get. If your cat has fatty liver disease, give her a high-protein diet because she'll use the extra protein, rather than fat, as an energy source.

Cancer

Regardless of the type of cancer your cat has, diet will go a long way toward keeping her strong. Research suggests that cats with cancer should be fed:

- a high-quality protein from meat sources
- a low-carbohydrate diet, with no grains and with vegetables making up no more than 5 percent of the diet
- a moderate-fat amount
- soluble and insoluble fiber; a mix of psyllium, pumpkin, and peas is best but you can substitute rice bran or beet pulp if necessary
- omega-3 essential fatty acids in the form of wild salmon oil.

Heart Problems

Heart disease affects both young and old cats and can occur alongside or as a result of other conditions, such as hyperthyroidism, kidney disease, and hypertension. If your cat has been diagnosed with a heart condition, take the following steps:

- Keep her sodium levels as low as possible; inspect treats and supplement labels carefully for sodium amounts.
- Feed her celery because animal studies have shown that its active compound, phthalide, relaxes the muscles of the arteries that regulate blood pressure, allowing these vessels to dilate; it also has a mild diuretic action.
- Add an extra 500 mg per day of the amino acid taurine.
- Add 10 mg per three pounds (1.4 kg) of body weight of the antioxidant coenzyme Q10.

Properly nourished cats save not only heartbreak but also veterinary bills. Tweak the recipes in this chapter as you deem necessary, bearing in mind that cats don't require grains and must eat a primarily fresh, raw-meat–based diet. Some cats handle vegetables just fine, but others might not be able to handle certain or all vegetables. Let your cats' needs guide how much meat, vegetable sources, and supplements to include in their diets. Remember that raw meat is a cat's natural diet, and a variety of meats will keep your cats happy and healthy.

Part Two: Wellness

As discussed in part one of this book, the key ingredient to whole health is prevention. But basic care and nutrition alone won't exempt your cat from occasional medical issues. Part two explores how to achieve total wellness through routine veterinary care and natural, at-home remedies. And, because physical and mental issues often become intertwined, Part two also covers the behavioral issues that can result from stress and anxiety or physical conditions. With you and a caring veterinarian working as team, you can use this section to deal with the health and behavioral issues your cats will face throughout their lives to provide them with years of health and happiness.

CHAPTER FOUR

Routine Veterinary Care

"Anyone who considers protocol

unimportant has never dealt with a cat."

ROBERT A. HEINLEIN

ood veterinary care is vital to your cat's well being. Your cat needs his human family and his veterinarian to be partners in his care. A kind, competent veterinarian serves as an invaluable resource in maintaining your cat's health. This chapter outlines some of the issues to keep in mind when it comes to your cat's health care, including making various health care decisions and procedures. As your cat's health care advocate, work closely with your veterinarian, and try your best to keep current with issues in cat health care.

To make your cat less anxious, speak soothingly to him while his veterinarian gives him a checkup.

Choosing a Veterinarian

To keep your cat in tip-top condition, make sure he receives periodic wellness checks. Establish a relationship with a veterinarian before health issues become an issue. You can use the same basic criteria to select a veterinarian that you would to choose your own medical doctor. Use the following questions to help you make your decision.

- Do I want a veterinarian close to my home?
- What are the clinic's hours of operation?
- Are they open on weekends and/or late in the evening?
- Do they provide emergency or after-hours care?
- Are the facilities up to date?
- Is the facility clean and sanitary?
- Do I want an office with one veterinarian, or do I prefer a multiveterinarian practice?
- Does the veterinarian have a nice bedside manner?
- Are specialists available at my veterinarian's facility, or will I have to go elsewhere for specialized services?
- How much does the veterinarian charge for office visits and services provided?
- When does the office expect payment, and what sources of payment do they accept?
- If I ever need to leave my cat at the clinic overnight, will someone be there to ensure my cat is all right?
- How friendly is the staff—the receptionist, veterinarian technicians, and assistants?
- Does my cat like this particular veterinarian and the staff?
- Does my veterinarian keep up with feline nutritional and health care information?
- Do I want an allopathic or holistic veterinarian (see page 92)?
- Do I want a feline-only practice (see page 94)?

If you have trouble with technical veterinary jargon, don't hesitate to ask your veterinarian to use layman's terms.

These questions should help you select a veterinarian both you and your cat will be happy with. If your cat gets sick in the car, for instance, having a nearby veterinarian might be one of the most important criteria for you, just for pragmatic reasons.

House-Call Veterinarians

Some veterinarians will come to your home to treat your cat and will draw blood, conduct checkups, and administer simple treatments. A veterinarian with a mobile clinic may perform minor surgery, depending on the laws in your state and county. For complicated procedures, your veterinarian can refer your cat to a specialty clinic.

You should consider a house-call veterinarian if you have a:

- cat that gets car sick
- cat that gets stressed out during a car ride or at the veterinarian's office
- cat that doesn't like other animals
- cat that's scared of humans, such as a former feral cat unused to much human contact
- large, multicat household
- physical problem that prevents you from taking your cat to a veterinarian.

Cats pick up on negative emotions and vibes so always listen to your cat; if he gets particularly stressed out going to a certain veterinarian's office, there might be something to it. Some cats get upset no matter how wonderful the veterinarian or the staff; in such cases, make sure you're otherwise happy with the veterinary clinic. Chapters six contains suggestions for using hydrosol and flower essence to help calm cats who get upset at veterinarian visits and car rides in general.

Your ultimate goal should be to find a veterinarian who gets along with both you and your cat. Your veterinarian should show kindness and caring toward your cat, but not shut you out if you have questions or concerns regarding your cat's care. One of the most rewarding relationships you can have as a cat caregiver is a partnership with a wonderful veterinarian, whether holistic or traditional.

If you can't locate a holistic veterinarian who meets your criteria, look for a traditional or allopathic veterinarian who believes in preventive care. If you're new to an area, get a personal recommendation from co-workers or neighbors. Visit the clinic if you can so you can get a better idea of whether the facility will meet your cats' needs.

Veterinarians around the world tend to fall under the category of either "traditional" or "allopathic." The various medical dictionaries seem to agree that the term "allopathy" first entered the lexicon in 1842. The father of homeopathy, Dr. Samuel Hahnemann, is credited with coining the term "allopathy" to denote the practice of medicine that treats disease with remedies that produce effects different from those produced by the disease under treatment. Most medical and veterinary schools teach this system of medicine for humans and animals, respectively.

Dr. Hahnemann codified a system of healing that he referred to as homeopathy. Homeopathy heals by gently stimulating the body's own immune response to a disease. Homeopaths give small doses,

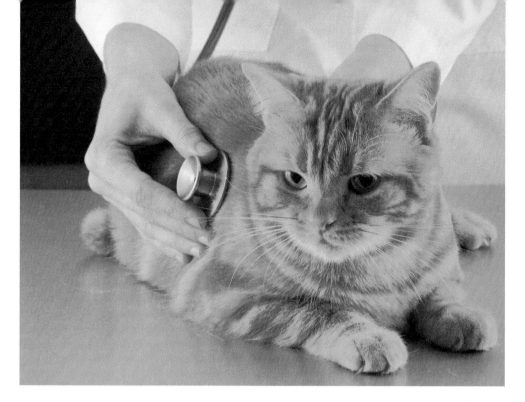

even infinitesimal in some cases, of the same substance that is causing the disease. In other words, homeopathy believes that like cures like.

If a cat suffers from autumn allergies, for example, his body's mast cells would release a chemical known as histamine. An allopath would prescribe antihistamines because they block histamine production, bringing about relief from symptoms. A homeopath would use a remedy that produces the same symptoms as ragweed allergies. One such remedy is *Ambrosia*, which is prepared from ragweed and mimics the symptoms of ragweed allergies. In small amounts, the body grows accustomed to ragweed, and the over-response from the immune system stops or at least slows down. The cat can then get through this and possibly even future ragweed seasons without any symptoms or side effects.

Homeopathy comes under the umbrella term "holistic." Holistic techniques, or modalities as they're often called, include the use of herbs, flower essences, reiki (a form of energy healing), chiropractic adjustments, homeopathy, acupuncture, allergy treatments (such as Nambudripad's Allergy Elimination Technique, or NAET), massage, and much more. Some holistic veterinarians continue to

A thorough checkup, including listening to your cat's heart, is vital to determine your cat's health.

offer diagnostic procedures such as X-rays, blood tests, and in some cases even surgery; others don't. Holistic veterinarians also usually consider diet extremely important, and many believe in species-appropriate, raw-meat–based diets for companion animals.

If you can't find a holistic veterinarian nearby, consider a team approach. For example, you can take your cat to an allopathic or traditional veterinarian locally and consult with a holistic veterinarian by email or over the phone. Needless to say, this would preclude such treatments as acupuncture, NAET, massage, and adjustments, but it would still let you have homeopathic and nutritional consults over the phone.

Feline-Only or Mixed Practice?

In many countries, veterinarians can get certification in the specialized care and treatment of cats. This isn't to say that other veterinarians don't keep up with current cat research, just that feline-only veterinarians are required to. Other mixed-practice veterinarians deal with several species, not all of which might be alike. So make sure your veterinarian stays current on cat research, regardless of whether your vet has a feline-only or mixed practice.

Despite a feline-only veterinarian's knowledge level, if the other items on your checklist don't mesh, you might be better off with a multispecies veterinarian with a small-animal specialty. For example, if the feline-only veterinarian doesn't stay open late in the evenings, and that's the only time you can take your cat in, then going to a feline-only veterinarian won't be possible.

As long as the practice meets your other criteria, such as hours of operation, close proximity, and other factors, you might want to consider a feline-only practice, particularly if you or your cats don't want the stress of other animals in the waiting room and if you have concerns about the special physiology of cats. Especially consider it if going to a cat-only practice would produce less stress for your cat, because stress can be so harmful to cats.

Cats' Unique Physiological Needs

Cats are unlike any other species, and because most medical studies use rats, which are closer to humans in physiology than to cats, it becomes not only difficult but unsafe to extrapolate findings from these studies. Because of their unique physiology, cats metabolize substances in different ways. Unfortunately, many medicines, herbs, and supplements considered safe for humans and other species can cause serious damage to cats, even killing them in some cases.

What's frustrating is that even with supplements generally considered safe, we still don't know the amounts cats can safely metabolize. For example, it was recently discovered that cats are ten times as sensitive as other species to the supplement alpha lipoic acid, an antioxidant supplement good for humans and most other species with diabetes, cancer, and other illnesses. Cats should get no more than 15 mg of alpha lipoic acid per pound (0.45 kg) of body weight.

Cats' bodies take a lot longer than humans' to detoxify salicylic acid and blood thinners that contain coumarin, morphine, and certain sulfonamides. Talk to your veterinarian about the possible effects of these ingredients if you see them listed on any medication or supplement your cat may have been prescribed.

Veterinarians are responsible for keeping current with research for all animals, including cats, but it never hurts to pay attention yourself. Keep an ear to the ground in case a supplement, herb, or drug previously thought safe is now considered harmful to cats based on new research data. To help you deal with this potential minefield, start with the assumption that, unless cats have eaten or ingested a substance for years—such as small birds and animals, the herb catnip, and the amino acid taurine, abundant in mice bodies—you should approach it with caution. You can keep up with current thinking with online discussion groups, mailing lists, and websites on holistic cat care.

Drugs and Other Medications

All the remedies in this book have been researched thoroughly and are safe for cats. However, don't assume that a product marketed for cats is automatically safe. Products marketed for pets in general or both dogs and cats warrant even more scrutiny because a large percentage of products safe for dogs are quite dangerous for cats. Use the lists provided in this chapter to ferret out products safe for cats, keeping in mind a "less is more" approach—always best when it comes to cats.

DON'T LET YOUR CAT INGEST THE FOLLOWING:

■ **paracetamol or acetaminophen (sold over the counter as Tylenol):** can cause death

■ **ibuprofen (sold as Motrin, Advil, Nuprin, and other anti-inflammatory brands):** can cause bleeding disorders and kidney failure

■ **naproxen (sold under the name Aleve):** can cause bleeding disorders and kidney failure

■ **phosphate enemas (sold in drugstores under such names as Fleet):** can cause death

■ **phenazopyridine:** pain medication used for urinary infections in humans that can cause hyperventilation and death in cats; no antidote

■ **benzocaine (a topical anesthetic):** can cause methemoglobinemia, which reduces oxygen capacity in blood

■ **over-the-counter antidiarrheal medications:** contain salicylates-can cause renal failure and bleeding

UNDERSTANDING COMMON MEDICATIONS:

■ **aspirin:** Don't allow more than one baby aspirin or $1/4$ adult tablet every three days; because cats metabolize this very slowly, it can build up quickly to toxic levels.

■ **prescription nonsteroidal anti-inflammatory agents:** These are given to cats for pain, but watch carefully because they can cause severe digestive upset and gastric ulcers.

■ **ovaban or other hormones:** These are prescribed for pain and excessive licking, but they've been implicated in breast cancer and diabetes.

■ **steroids such as prednisone:** These are prescribed for a variety of conditions, including asthma and allergies, but even a single round has been implicated in diabetes. Long-term use has serious adverse effects on the immune system.

■ **ammonium chloride and the amino acid L-methionine (prescribed as urinary acidifiers):** You can use these short-term to bring your cat's pH level to the ideal number; avoid long-term use because they can cause urine to become too acidic and contribute to calcium oxalate crystal formation.

Note: Some antibiotics can cause more problems than others, so keep track of this information to share with your cat's veterinarian in case your cat needs an antibiotic. If your cat must take any antibiotic, give her acidophilus during and at least a week following the course of medication to help repopulate her stomach with good bacteria.

HERBS THAT ARE NEVER SAFE TO USE INTERNALLY OR EXTERNALLY:

- alfalfa
- arnica
- bloodroot
- boneset
- borage
- chapparal
- coltsfoot
- comfrey
- elecampane
- garlic
- lily of the valley
- lobelia
- mandrake
- meadowsweet
- red clover
- rue
- white willow bark
- wormwood

DANGEROUS HOUSEHOLD PRODUCTS:

- antifreeze (contains ethylene glycol): can cause kidney failure
- cleansers and spray containing pine oil, phenol, cresol, or chloroxylenols: can cause poisoning
- insecticides and pesticides (including rat poison) containing pyrethrins, strychnine, and organophosphates: can cause damage to the central nervous system

DANGEROUS AND DEADLY PLANTS:

Various animal welfare and cat fancier organizations provide free booklets containing long lists of plants that can cause serious problems, including vomiting, diarrhea, and other intestinal problems. These three plants, however, are particularly dangerous because they can kill a cat in short order.

- dieffenbachia
- Easter lily, tiger lily, and other varieties of lilies
- oleander

Wellness Checks

Routine health care should consist of annual wellness checks, which involve a physical exam, a urinalysis, and possibly examination of a fecal sample. By keeping tabs on your cat's health and feeding him a healthy diet, your veterinarian bills should be far lower than they would be otherwise. After you've selected a health care professional, establish an appointment schedule that fits your budget.

Some pet health insurance companies now cover preventative care, so look into purchasing such a policy for your cat. If you find the cost of health care prohibitive, consider that some veterinarians have a sliding scale and will negotiate lower fees; you can also contact your local veterinary school to see if they offer reduced rates.

Some cats like to sleep in their carriers, often choosing them over plush cat beds.

Getting Ready for a Veterinary Visit

If possible, bring a fecal and urine sample with you when you take your cat to the veterinarian for his annual wellness check. All you need is 3 to 5 ml of urine, which you can put in any small, clean container, and a fingernail-size sample of stool in a plastic bag. Your veterinarian can provide you with urine containers and fecal samplers. You can refrigerate urine and fecal samples for up to twelve hours before you go to the veterinarian's office.

To make the experience as pleasant as possible, bring your cat's carrier out the day before the visit and spray the inside with a pheromone product available at most pet supply stores. Spray a towel with lavender hydrosol or catnip spray or both, and place the towel inside the carrier. Leave the door to the carrier open so that it will pique your cat's curiosity.

On the day of the visit, chances are good that your sweet, unsuspecting cat will already be curled up in the carrier. If not, place him in the carrier, and the combination of pheromones and hydrosols will keep him relaxed during the dreaded car ride. About half an hour before leaving the house, or even first thing in the morning, give your cat a flower essence. You can dab it on his paw pads or ears or add it to his drinking water. Some essences that work well for this are Aspen for fear of the unknown, Rock Rose for trauma, or a combination calming essence. You can continue to dose him with these if he becomes upset when you get to the veterinarian's office.

At the Veterinarian's Office

Your cat will be able to smell other animals in the reception area, but the pleasant, calming smells inside the carrier will help reduce his anxiety. If at all possible, sit away from other species of animals, and keep your cat's carrier facing toward you. This will let you speak to your cat soothingly and keep him calm while waiting for the veterinarian.

At an annual examination, your vet should check the following:

- weight, temperature, and heart and pulse rate
- eyes for discharge
- ears for mites and fungal infections and growths
- coat for fleas and ringworm
- kidneys, liver and abdomen abnormalities
- heart abnormalities
- teeth for tartar and gums for swelling

Pheromones

Cats have a tendency to rub their faces on various items and, by doing so, spreading feline facial pheromone on the area as well as on their human's body and clothing to mark the human or item as belonging to the cat. When cats smell areas around the house that they've marked, they feel more relaxed and at home. Cats are also less likely to spray areas they've marked with their facial pheromones.

One of the more recent and exciting developments in the cat world has been the commercial availability of pheromone-derived products for home use. At least one brand of cat pheromones comes in a spray form as well as a plug-in diffuser. This type of product can help cats in all sorts of situations; it can help reduce stress, deter spraying, and promote a general sense of well-being. You can spray pheromone products onto surfaces where your cat is likely to rub his cheeks as well as on the inside of his cat carrier before a veterinarian visit. You can also spray them on a cat's bedding or plug a diffuser in the room where you keep the litter box.

Schedule	Procedure
2 months old	Feline panleukopenia virus (FPV) vaccine (distemper shot) Fecal test
3 months old	FPV booster vaccine
4 months old	Rabies vaccine with booster one year later for cat healthy enough to receive it
12 months old	Blood test to determine baseline

After age one, cats can typically move to an annual wellness check with urinalysis. Depending on the outdoor risks where you live, consider a rabies shot every three years, as well as regular fecal tests if your cat goes outside.

Vaccinations

Opinions on vaccinations range from those who believe that vaccines don't work, suppress cats' immunity, and cause health problems to those who believe vaccinations prevent life-threatening diseases and must be given every year. The issue of overvaccination has been a hot topic in veterinary circles for some time now as more traditional veterinarians question the need for annual vaccinations.

If your cat spends most of his time indoors, he has a low likelihood of being exposed to disease, which may allow you to follow a less aggressive vaccination schedule.

What Are Vaccines, and Does My Cat Really Need Them?

Vaccines are supposed to work by stimulating the body's defense system to produce antibodies that help fight off invading viruses. In theory, injecting a small amount of a disease-causing virus, such as rabies or the respiratory virus calici, will stimulate the cat's immune response to the virus so that when the real virus tries to invade, the body recognizes it, not allowing it to cause disease. At this time, most veterinary schools advocate a three-year revaccination schedule, not routine annual booster shots.

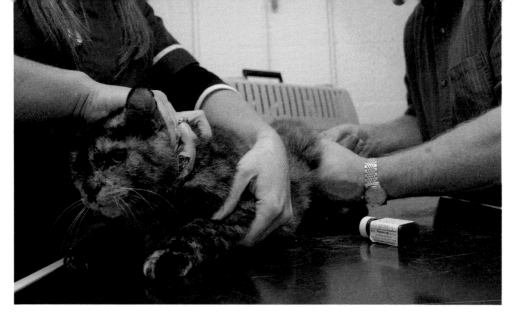

To help reduce stress levels prior to blood drawing and other veterinary procedures, let your cat sniff lavender hydrosol or dab a combination of calming flower essence on his paw pads.

Over-vaccination can cause potentially life-threatening cancerous tumors at the injection site. The risk of developing these vaccine-associated sarcomas just isn't worth the minimal benefit of booster shots each year. When you have your cat vaccinated, ask your veterinarian not to administer the vaccines between the shoulder blades because removal of a cancerous lump from this area is extremely difficult.

Different Types of Vaccines

Generally speaking, there are three types of vaccines: live, modified-live, and killed; most cat vaccines fall into the modified-live category, although there are at least three killed vaccines in use. All three types of vaccines work the same way, but they're prepared differently. There's a lot of controversy about their use and side effects. Several strains of vaccines still under research are considered lower risk, such as transdermal, oral, and intranasal vaccine preparations; ask your veterinarian about these options.

At this time, only the rabies (VRCP) and feline leukemia virus (FeLV) vaccine use a killed virus; the others use modified-live viruses. A killed vaccine needs the addition of an adjuvant to give the immune system a poke because it doesn't contain the virus that the live ones do. Unfortunately, it's these adjuvants that cause tumors at the injection site. One of the culprits is aluminum hydroxide used in the adjuvant material. After your cat gets either of these two killed vaccines, watch for pain and swelling at the injection site. If swelling doesn't go down in a few days, take your cat to the veterinarian to determine if he has a cancerous lump at the site. Never ignore a lump at an injection site because this is a very invasive form of cancer, and early attention might make the difference between your cat losing a leg rather than his life.

Even a modified-live virus contains tiny amounts of the actual virus and can cause mild symptoms of the disease. Some cats can have an allergic reaction to these vaccines. Such a reaction typically occurs between half an hour and twenty-four hours after administration and can be life-threatening. Anaphylactic reactions come on quickly; symptoms to watch for are vomiting and agitation. If your cat has these sudden, violent symptoms, he'll need immediate veterinary care because such reactions can be fatal. Watch for other adverse reactions following administration as well, including mild fever, weakness, lethargy, decreased appetite, swelling, sneezing, joint pain, and eye and motor problems.

Risk versus Reward

Ultimately it boils down to risk versus reward. The two vaccines most likely to cause cancer at the injection site are FeLV and rabies. Because both diseases are transmitted through direct contact with an infected animal, the risk for indoor-only cats greatly outweighs the reward. The development of a malignant tumor at injection site—five out of every 10,000 vaccinated cats—is most likely for FeLV and rabies vaccines.

If you decide to vaccinate your cat, avoid combination vaccines, also known as multivalents, because they involve too many antigens going into your cat at one time. No matter the type of vaccinations, always be on the lookout for adverse side effects.

If you purchase your cat from a breeder, be sure to obtain documentation of her kitten shots.

So What Should a Cat Caregiver Do?

Consider a minimalist approach, and give the bare minimum vaccines necessary—kitten shots with one booster, and no other vaccinations ever. It's not just people in the holistic community who believe that vaccines carry a great deal of risk; mainstream veterinarians are following a more conservative protocol, administering only the vaccines absolutely necessary to each particular cat's health condition.

In his book *The Nature of Animal Healing*, Dr. Martin Goldstein recommends only one vaccine for indoor cats. He suggests giving kittens at ten to twelve weeks of age a single, not combination vaccine—the feline panleukopenia (FPV) vaccine because it's the only vaccine proven somewhat effective, with fewer negative effects than other vaccines. For outdoor cats, he recommends one rabies shot with no boosters because a single shot has been shown to protect a cat for life.

If you feel concerned about giving only one rabies shot and one FPV shot to your kitten, you can give the 4-in-1 kitten combination, also known as the "kitten series of shots" with one booster, and that's it. You don't need to give any more annual or even periodic vaccinations; your cat should be immunized for the rest of his life. Dr. Hamilton, a veterinary homeopath and author of *Small Doses for Small Animals: Homeopathy for Cats and Dogs*, concurs with Dr. Goldstein and suggests a single FPV shot for kittens and then a single rabies shot if you must meet a legal requirement for the shot. In his book, he discusses how unnecessary and risky boosters are. Holistic veterinarians

Kitty Vaccines

A standard "kitten shot" consists of a 4-in-1 vaccine to inoculate against the following respiratory diseases:

- feline calicivirus

- feline herpes virus, formerly known as feline rhinotracheitis virus

- FPV, also known as feline distemper

- chlamydia

Of these four vaccines, the FPV vaccine is the most effective and long lasting, with a lot fewer side effects than the other three in the combination vaccine. As discussed in this chapter, you must weigh the benefit of the other vaccines commonly given to kittens and cats, such as FeLV and rabies, against the risks.

Drs. Pitcairn, Goldstein, and Hamilton discuss this as well as the negative long-term effects of vaccines in their books. If you're concerned about the issue of vaccination, these books are a great resource.

Outdoor cats should be vaccinated against rabies because they are at the most risk of being bitten by a carrier animal—bats, raccoons, skunks, or other infected cats. Rabies is the only vaccination mandated by law, but that can vary, even by county within the same state. The label on all vaccines state that only healthy animals can receive them, so ask your veterinarian for an exemption if your cat isn't completely healthy. A cat with a compromised immune system, for instance, should never receive a vaccine, which would include cats with FeLV, FIP, or FIV and cats suffering from an upper respiratory illness. Cats undergoing cancer treatment and cats running a fever above 103°F (39°C) shouldn't receive vaccines. Never give a pregnant cat a vaccine because it can cause serious birth defects.

Spaying and Neutering

Unless you're a breeder, you should plan on getting your cats spayed or neutered. Female cats are spayed and male cats are neutered. Contrary to myth, altering your cat won't cause him or her to develop urinary problems, become lazy, or gain weight. Your cat will actually become even more affectionate after being fixed, and will be a much happier cat.

When to Spay or Neuter

Neutering involves removal of the testes so the male cat no longer produces sperm. It's a less involved procedure and so usually costs less than spaying. Your male cat won't need to be under anesthesia too long and should bounce back from it faster for this reason.

Neuter male cats after the testicles descend but before they reach six months of age or else they're more likely to spray or mark their territory. As your male kitten gets older, the odor of his urine will become more pungent. Get him neutered as soon as his urine starts to smell strongly, because he's more likely to begin spraying at this point. Once a cat starts spraying, even neutering might not make him stop because it will switch from a physical to a behavioral issue.

Spaying involves removal of the uterus, fallopian tubes, and ovaries. Your cat will be put under general anesthesia, so one rule of thumb is to wait until she's a safe weight—two pounds (0.9 kg)—before having this surgery performed. Also, because your cats excrete the drugs and gas used for anesthesia through the kidneys and liver, your cat's organs must be developed and functioning properly so her health won't be compromised.

Some cats can go into heat as young as three months, so plan on getting your cat spayed between three and four months of age. If, however, she goes into heat earlier than that, make an appointment with her veterinarian right away; some veterinarians are trained to spay kittens that are as young as seven or eight weeks old.

WHAT CAN HAPPEN IF I DON'T SPAY OR NEUTER MY CATS?

Beside the obvious risk of pregnancy, failure to spay or neuter a cat carries other risks.

Males:

- more likely to spray to mark his territory
- more likely to get into fights to protect his territory, possibly resulting in nasty cuts and bruises, which may get infected because cat claws harbor bacteria
- more likely to of develop testicular cancer

Females:

- has higher risk of developing mammary tumors and cancers of the reproductive system
- is at risk for uterine infections called pyometra, which spayed cats don't get
- may develop marking behavior
- will undergo stressful heat cycles

How to Give a Cat a Pill

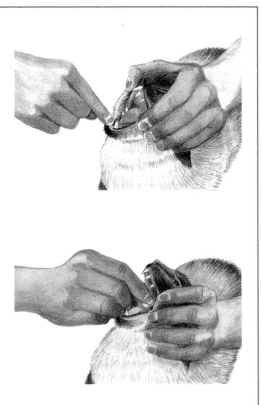

1. **Face your cat forward, either by placing him on a countertop or kneeling on the floor with his body between your knees, using gentle pressure to keep him securely tucked in. If your cat is likely to use his claws, make sure your knees block his front legs. Crossing your ankles is very useful, too, because it blocks your cat's other escape route— from behind.**

2. **Encircle your cat's head from the top by placing the palm of your hand between his ears and your thumb and middle finger on either side of his mouth. Apply gentle pressure on both sides of his mouth and tilt his head back a little so his eyes are looking at the ceiling. This should cause his mouth to open slightly.**

3. **Try and deposit the pill on his tongue as far back as you can. If you stroke his throat, he will swallow as a reflex, swallowing the pill as well.**

4. **Once you see your cat's tongue, the pill has gone down.**

TIPS FOR GIVING YOUR CAT A PILL

- Look for a long pill dispenser that has a plunger handle and plastic tines on the end so pills fit inside without falling out.
- Some people find blowing on their cat's face ever so lightly makes them blink and swallow at the same time. Use your judgment because some cats might not appreciate this!
- When administering more than one pill or dealing with a pill that dissolves too quickly, you can use empty gelatin capsules in size 3, 4, or 5 and put the pills inside them. You can also reuse capsules that you empty into your cat's food.

- For hard-to-pill cats, try hiding the pill in a treat, such as baby food. If your cat is adept at eating around the pill, you can try crushing the tablet into a fine powder so you can mix it with a treat.
- To give a liquid medication, use a plastic syringe without a needle, and have a compounding pharmacy prepare the medication in fish or other meat flavor to make it more palatable to your cat.

Why Get Blood and Urine Tests?

You can learn a lot from testing a cats' urine. Because they're desert animals, cats ingest most of their moisture from food, not water, and produce concentrated urine. A useful, noninvasive technique, urinalysis can function as an early warning for health problems lurking in your cat. Urinalyses can provide information not only about the kidneys and bladder, but also the liver, pancreas, and other organs. Besides helping us make a diagnosis, urinalysis can guide a course of treatment. Based on the specific type of bacteria in the urine, the veterinarian might prescribe a particular type of antibiotic.

If your cat suffers from chronic urinary problems, you can easily monitor your cat's urinary pH level at home. This will save you money and your cat the stress of regular trips to the veterinarian's office. You can buy urine testing strips for pH testing, an inexpensive way to keep track of your cat's urinary pH. Urine that's too acidic or too alkaline is a warning sign you shouldn't ignore.

Blood tests provide useful information about your cat's kidney and liver function, as well as hydration and protein levels, status of the bone marrow and anemia, as well as his immune system. Ask your veterinarian's office for a copy of your cat's blood and urine test results. Your veterinarian should go over any high and low values on both the blood test and urinalysis. Keep a file containing all your cat's records and medical history for reference.

Turmeric Test

Cats' urine pH should ideally range from 6.0 to 6.5 and definitely no higher than 6.8. To ensure your cat's urine has not gone above this level, just dig around in your herb cabinet and find the yellow spice turmeric, a staple in Indian cooking. Mix $1/4$ teaspoon of turmeric powder into 5 ounces (150 ml) of rubbing alcohol. Let this mixture sit for a few minutes. Using a dropper, collect as much urine as you can from your cat's litter box. See tips for collecting a urine sample (page 146).

Drop a urine sample into a small shot glass or jar, along with an approximately equal amount of the turmeric and alcohol solution. If the solution turns red, your cat's urine has a pH higher than 6.8. You want the solution to remain yellow, which would indicate your cat's urine has a pH less than 6.8.

This quick home test tells you that your cat's urine isn't alkaline; it won't tell you if your cat's urine is too acidic, which could indicate a problem such as calcium oxalate stones. If you need to know how much lower or higher than 6.8 your cat's urinary pH is, you'll need a urine testing strip for pH.

Urine Testing Strips

You can test for quite a few things at home with a ten-parameter reagent strip that you can purchase online or in a drugstore. You only need a drop or two of urine on the strip. Try and get the sample as soon as your cat urinates because the longer the urine sits, the more alkaline it will become, giving you a less accurate reading. The reagent strip measures pH, glucose, protein, blood, ketones, nitrites, leuko-cytes, bilirubin, urobilinogen, and specific gravity.

To determine if your cat has stones or crystals, a technician trained in the procedure will test urinary sediment. This type of testing requires the use of a centrifuge and a microscope.

Parameter	Normal Results	What Abnormal Results Indicate
Specific Gravity ability;	1.015 to 1.05	Low results indicate loss of kidney's filtering fatty liver disease
pH	6.0 to 6.8 (ideally 6 to 6.5)	Acidic: acidifying diets, including prescription foods; use of urinary acidifiers Alkaline: grain- and/or vegetable-heavy diet; bacterial infection; measured after food, indicates postprandial alkaline tide
Glucose	Negative to trace	Positive: hyperglycemia or diabetes
Protein	Negative to trace	Trace: urinary infection; renal disease, especially if specific gravity is less than 1.020
Blood	Negative	Positive: infection, trauma, inflammation, bladder stones, or cancer
Bilirubin	Negative	Positive: liver disease; bile duct obstruction
Nitrite	Negative	Positive: bacterial infection
Leukocytes or white blood cells	Negative	Positive: urinary tract infection or white blood cells bladder infection

When your cat has a urinalysis at the veterinarian's office, ask to take a copy of the results home with you so you can review them. Although your veterinarian will make health care recommendations based on these results, remember that as the medical advocate for your cat, you should have a working knowledge of his overall health, and the results of the urinalysis can tell you a lot.

- Color: Normal urine is amber-yellow in color and ranges from clear to slightly cloudy in appearance. The more concentrated the urine, the darker the color. Blood in the urine gives it a red-brown tinge; white blood cells (WBCs) can make the urine cloudy.
- pH : This measures the acidity or alkalinity of urine. A pH of 7.0 is neutral, but in the case of cats, a slightly acidic pH—specifically, a pH between 6.0 and 6.5—is ideal. Meat produces more acidic urine, and grains have an alkalizing effect on

urine. Feeding a species-appropriate diet should help maintain your cat's urine at the correct pH.

- Specific gravity (SG): This determines how well your cat is concentrating his urine. An SG of 1.035 or higher is ideal because cats have fairly concentrated urine. Cats with kidney insufficiency have dilute urine because nephrons in their kidneys are lost. Most cats with fatty liver disease, also known as hepatic lipidosis, have an SG of less than 1.020.
- Protein: Normal urine shouldn't have any detectable protein in it. Small amounts of protein in dilute urine are very significant because it indicates a loss of kidney function.
- Glucose: Not normally present in urine, glucose may indicate the possibility of diabetes. However, several causes, including stress, can elevate glucose levels in the urine, so have any suspicious test results be repeated and verified by a blood glucose test.
- Blood: Urine shouldn't contain any blood. Blood in the urine can indicate an infection, kidney stones, trauma, or bleeding from a tumor in the urinary system.
- Bilirubin: Normally, urine contains no bilirubin or urobilinogen. Both are pigments cleared by the liver; presence of either is a marker for liver disease or bile duct obstruction.
- Nitrate: The presence of nitrate should indicate a UTI, but this is a notoriously inaccurate test.
- WBCs: Larger than normal numbers of WBCs can indicate inflammation from stones or a bladder infection.
- Bacteria: If the sample isn't sterile, it can contain small amounts of bacteria. However, large amounts of bacteria indicate a bladder infection, especially if the sample is sterile. If the sample has a high bacteria count, your cat will need a urine culture-and-sensitivity test to determine the specific type of bacteria present. This is important because it drives the choice of antibiotic; different antibiotics target different bacteria.
- Crystals: Cats' urine sometimes contains tiny crystals. In cats, the most common type is struvite, followed by calcium oxalate and ammonium urate. When crystals clump together, they form stones in the bladder called uroliths. A dry or kibble diet is more likely to cause crystal formation because it produces overly concentrated urine. An overly alkaline diet promotes sturvite stone formation, whereas urine that's too acidic can lead to calcium oxalate stones.

Problems That Call For Immediate Veterinary Care

■ animal attack

■ blood in urine

■ burns

■ bloody diarrhea and/or vomiting, with or without foul odor

■ car or other vehicle hitting cat

■ cold extremities, especially with heart problems, because the cat might have thrown a blood clot

■ collapse or loss of balance, including staggering or walking in circles

■ continued vomiting, especially if vomit contains blood

■ convulsions or seizures accompanied by muscle tremors or dilated pupils

■ cut greater than a $1/4$ inch (0.6 cm) deep or with bone exposed

■ difficulty breathing, including rapid breathing, coughing, or choking

■ eye problems: a puncture wound; sudden redness in the eye (especially if your cat has kidney failure because this could mean retinal detachment); scratched cornea; squinting and third eyelid prolapse

■ fracture or any suspicion of broken bones

■ frostbite or hypothermia

■ great pain

■ ingestion of poisonous material or medication

■ limping, sprain, or lameness

■ lump or tumor: could be cancerous

■ nonresponsive or comatose state

■ straining continually in the litter box but unable to pass stool or urinate

■ uncontrollable bleeding from any part of the body: don't attempt to apply a tourniquet; instead, apply pressure to stop bleeding while taking cat to the veterinarian.

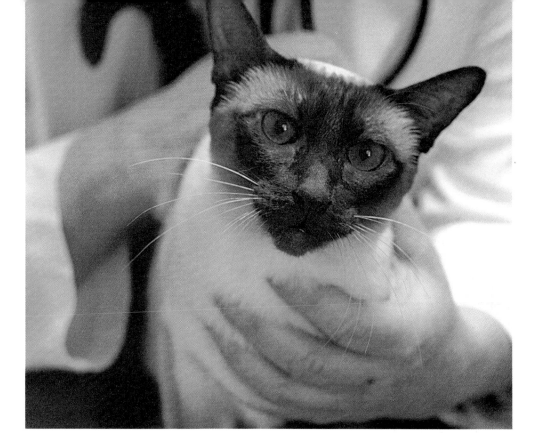

If you're lucky enough to have a cat enter your life as a kitten, get him accustomed to being handled through frequent and regular grooming sessions, as laid out in chapter one. By keeping his eyes and ears clean, his coat mat-free, and his gums and teeth in good shape, you'll be proactive and able to determine when he might need to visit a veterinarian. Sometimes you can take matters into your hands and treat minor ailments at home through the judicious use of alternative therapies.

In addition to other negative effects, stress can cause elevated readings on blood and urine tests.

CHAPTER FIVE

Home Care and Minor Ailments

"Cats are rather delicate creatures and they are subject to a good many ailments, but I never heard of one who suffered from insomnia."

JOSEPH WOOD KRUTCH

This chapter discusses gentle alternative medicine modalities, such as homeopathy, herbs, flower essences, and floral waters, that cat caregivers can administer at home. You'll learn about different modalities that you may want to investigate and study in more depth yourself. For other modalities, such as acupuncture, NAET, and chiropractics, you'll need to consult with the appropriate health care professionals.

Aromatherapy

The oil extracted from a plant's bark, seed, root, or fruit is known as essential oil. The most commonly used extraction process, involving distillation with heated water, yields two products: the essential oil and the condensed water produced from steam. The latter is known as plant water essence (not to be confused with flower essences) as well as other names, including hydrosol, hydrolat, floral water, hydroflorate, and distillate. Hydrosols in their true form contain all the therapeutic properties of the plant. You can safely use hydrosols on cats, but never use essential oils either topically or internally; they're very dangerous for cats.

You shouldn't use essential oils on or around cats because they contain hydrocarbons or terpenes, which cats' livers have trouble metabolizing. Cats' livers can't excrete these substances because they lack a key enzyme humans have that allows us to eliminate the particular terpenoid compounds present in essential oils through body waste.

You might not notice a problem right away, but the harmful effects of essential oils can build up over time and cause serious problems for your cat. Cats can absorb external applications through their thin skins, which can build up to dangerous levels in their bodies; in some cases essential oils can burn their skin. Never use essentials oils on your cats, regardless of where you read such a recommendation.

Also, don't use essential oils or synthetic fragrance oils in an inhaler, diffuser, or humidifier around cats because the volatile oils can enter cats' lungs and cause damage, both in the lungs and the liver, from the buildup of these materials to toxic levels. Avoid commercial plug-in oil diffusers for the same reasons.

If you absolutely must use essential oils for yourself or your family, do so in a room your cat doesn't use, and even then, make sure the room has proper ventilation in case your cat ventures into this room.

Signs of essential oil toxicity include lethargy, lack of coordination, dehydration, paralysis, vomiting, drooling, and other common signs of poisoning. At least one study documents poisoning from tea tree oil in three Angora cats. Because we now know a little more about the negative effects of essential oils on cats, it's safer to simply avoid them.

Although cats can't tolerate essential oils, they can still get the benefits of aromatherapy using hydrosols or floral waters. Hydrosols are a safe and gentle alternative to essential oils because they offer much of the same benefits with none of the toxicity. You can use them they way you would a linen spray—one or two sprays of lavender hydrosol on your cat's bedding or carrier, for example, will help calm her down.

Because pure hydrosols don't contain preservatives, you'll need to refrigerate them. Check your bottle and make sure it's pure hydrosol, and not plain water mixed with essential oil; some companies might sell this under the guise of floral water. For any external recipe provided in this book, you can substitute pure hydrosol for plain water if needed.

Because hydrosols have the same therapeutic qualities as their corresponding essential oil, you can use hydrosols on your cats based on the essential oil's healing properties. The table on page 117 lists problems your cat may develop and which commonly available hydrosols you can use to help her. You can spray hydrosols onto your cat's bedding or carrier, or in the air. You can also dab them on your cat's paw pads, inside her ear, and on her skin. However, cats typically aren't fond of sprays because of the hissing sound they make, so first spray some mist onto gauze or a lint-free cotton pad and then apply on your cat.

As far as we know, hydrosols are safe for cats, but always keep in mind that as we learn more about cats, we may discover that something we thought of as safe can cause problems. No definitive data exists on the internal use of hydrosols for cats.

With their excellent sense of smell, cats can benefit from scents like lavender, neroli, and rose. If you cannot find hydrosols, crush some dried flowers and place them in a sachet near your cat's bedding.

INDICATION	HYDROSOLS
Depression	Lavender, chamomile, rosemary
Dry skin	Rose, chamomile, sandalwood
Eye wash	Green myrtle
Feline acne	Melissa (also called lemon balm), lavender, witch hazel
Fleas	Lavender, rosemary, lemon verbena
Herpes	Melissa (lemon balm)
Inflammation	Witch hazel, melissa (lemon balm), cucumber, yarrow
Itching	Witch hazel, rose, cucumber
Loss of fur*	Rosemary
Scars	St. John's wort, helichrysum (also called immortelle or everlasting)
Skin irritation	Chamomile, geranium
Stress	Lavender, chamomile, neroli, catnip, rose
Sunburn	Yarrow, lavender
Wounds	Lavender, tea tree

* If the reason for this is stress-related, include other hydrosols that help with stress and also treat with flower essences.

Certain hydrosols such as yarrow and helichrysum have a rather strong, even what some might consider an unpleasant, scent. If you or your cats dislike the smell of a particular hydrosol, you can use a different hydrosol, because often more than one hydrosol works for each problem. If minimizing the smell makes the hydrosol tolerable, then mix it with another one that you do like, such as lavender or rose.

Herbs

Whether you think of herbs as leaves and other nonwoody parts of a plant or more loosely as all parts of plants and spices—flowers, leaves, stems, seeds, barks, roots, twigs, and fruits—there's little doubt about

Dangerous Herbs

Certain constituents in herbs are dangerous for cats; these should be listed in any general herb book. Broad categories of herbs to avoid are those containing pyrrolizidine alkaloids such as comfrey, anticoagulants coumarins such as red clover, and salicins such as meadowsweet and white willow bark. Other herbs such as wormwood, rue, and black walnut used for parasite control are harsh, so avoid giving them to your cats. A new valuable resource for cat lovers who want to keep up with herbal issues is the Veterinary Botanical Medicine Association. Their web address is www.vbma.org.

their powerful medicinal properties. When it comes to cats, however, our lack of knowledge of how cats metabolize plants, if at all, constrains us.

The safest thing to do with herbs is to treat them as you would a drug, and check herb sources for contraindications and side effects. Because there are no herbs poisonous to humans that are safe for cats, a good rule of thumb is to avoid all herbs with known complications, toxicity, or side effects in humans.

If ever in doubt, check the primary constituents of the herb, and if it contains salicin, coumarin, or pyrrolizidine alkaloids, avoid it. To help you navigate this potentially tricky area, this chapter contains two lists: one shows herbs that have a long history of use in cats and are generally safe for cats (make sure you follow the typical precautions for their use, even with humans), and the other shows herbs that have medicinal value in cats but that you should use with caution and only for the short term.

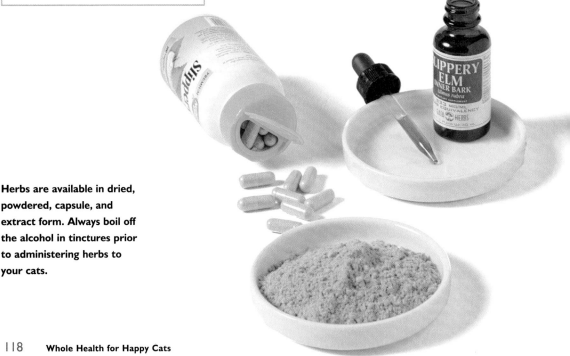

Herbs are available in dried, powdered, capsule, and extract form. Always boil off the alcohol in tinctures prior to administering herbs to your cats.

Herbs Currently Known To Be Safe if Used Short-Term for Medicinal Purposes

Although these herbs have some history of safety, always watch for problems such as lethargy, poor appetite, vomiting, digestive upset, or other negative reactions.

- andrographis paniculata for sinus problems
- arjuna, a cardiotonic
- astragalus, an immune booster
- blackberry for diarrhea
- boswellia for arthritis
- cayenne for arthritis
- cinnamon to lower blood glucose levels
- dandelion leaf and root, a diuretic that contains high levels of potassium
- echinacea, given at the first signs of a cold
- eldeberry for sinusitus
- fennel for digestive upset
- ginger for nausea
- ginkgo biloba, a blood thinner good for circulatory problems
- ginseng, American and Siberian, for the immune system and to combat colds
- goldenseal, an antibacterial
- hawthorne flowers and berries, a cardiotonic
- milk thistle for liver problems
- parsley, a diuretic that can cause potassium loss
- peppermint leaf for nausea and indigestion
- St. John's wort for depression
- valerian for appetite stimulation

Herbs Generally Recognized as Supportive and Safe for Cats

- **aloe vera gel (inner leaf)**
- **catnip**
- **cranberry**
- **marshmallow**
- **raspberry leaf**
- **slippery elm bark**
- **stinging nettles (for sneezing)**
- **turmeric or curcumin**

Herbs you should reserve for only a few days' use in a given year are uva ursi, kava kava, and licorice. Herbs you can apply externally for short-term use include yellow dock, Oregon grape root, eyebright, and chamomile. Your cat may ingest small amounts of these when she licks herself.

Various Chinese herbal formulas have also been used successfully in cats, such as Rehmannia 6, commonly referred to as Six Flavor Tea pills, for kidney complaints. Your holistic veterinarian can guide you in the use of these formulas. Be careful about using herbs in single form or in combinations you make up because these herbs have a long tradition of being used in certain combinations for good reason.

Also, be alert for combination herbal products sold by various manufacturers for health conditions. For example, heart formulas frequently contain guggul, which can potentially overstimulate the thyroid gland—not something cats typically need. Similarly, urinary formulas contain herbs good for breaking up the sort of stones humans get (calcium oxalate) or aren't appropriate for cats, such as uva ursi or juniper berries, which are too harsh for a cat's system.

Always give the body a rest from herbs, even safe ones. You can also alternate herbs with similar constituents, such as cranberry and blueberry for urinary problems, echinacea and astragalus for immune support, and marshmallow root and slippery elm bark for soothing the bladder and stomach. Above all, keep in mind that herbs aren't benign; their potent constituents have the capacity to harm cats if used inappropriately.

Homeopathy

The core philosophy of homeopathy is "similia similibus curentur" or "let like be cured with like." Although this principle was initially put forth by Hippocrates and later explored by the Swiss doctor Paracelsus, the German physician Samuel Hahnemann established in the 1790s the form of homeopathy that we follow today. Frustrated by the healing methods used at the time, such as blood letting, purgatives, and leeches, he explored a gentler approach to healing.

He experimented on himself by taking chinchona bark (which contains quinine), the cure for malaria, although he didn't have the disease.

He found that, after taking the bark, he soon devloped symptoms of malaria that lasted for several hours; the symptoms would go away when he stopped. He continued experimenting with other materials, including belladonna made from the deadly nightshade plant, with similar results.

For the remainder of his life, he continued to refine what he'd learned into a sophisticated system of healing. Dr. Hahnemann and his test subjects undertook "provings," which involved meticulously recording the overall sensation as well as the specific physical and mental symptoms experienced by healthy individuals when given minute amounts of a remedy.

These detailed provings have been compiled into various books called *Repertories*, which allow users to look up remedies that match their symptoms. The single remedy that matches a person's cluster of symptoms is the one that should be taken or given. To confirm that the remedy matches and to narrow down to a perfect match, you can read detailed remedy descriptions in a book called a *Materia Medica*. This may help because, at first blush, sometimes more than one remedy seems to match. Accounting for obvious differences, such as no symptoms for a third eyelid or tail, you can use a human repertory to determine the remedy for a cat.

How Are Homeopathic Remedies Prepared?

Homeopathic remedies were originally made from plant, animal, or mineral substances, but the choice of substances used to make remedies has expanded since the days of Dr. Hahnemann to include such things as body tissue to prepare sarcodes from healthy tissues and nosodes from diseased tissues. The preparer first extracts the medical constituents using alcohol to prepare the mother tincture—similar to an herbal extract. Then this mother tincture is diluted at various levels to prepare remedies. For example, a dilution of nine drops of water to one drop of mother tincture makes a 1X potency. This dilution is then succussed—forcefully struck against a firm surface, such as the palm of your hand or a book—because it's believed to transfer energy into the homeopathic solution.

To prepare a 2X potency, one drop of the 1X liquid is diluted with nine drops of water and then

Several companies sell homeopathy supply kits, which are an economical way to keep commonly used remedies on hand. Use the remedies in potencies of 30C or lower and only for the short term. You can give an initial remedy two or three times in the first hour or two, but only if it appears to be alleviating your cat's symptoms. Always take your cat to a veterinarian if symptoms don't go away quickly.

succussed. The technique for a C potency involves one drop of mother tincture diluted with ninety-nine drops of water. With each successive dilution and succussion, the remedy's potency increases. The higher a remedy's potency, the more powerful it is, and the more judiciously it should be used.

We prepare homeopathic remedies today much as they did in the late 1700s, except that now machines handle the series of dilutions and shaking. When the tincture reaches the desired potency, it's poured into a bottle of sugar tablets. To administer the remedy, either place one tablet or pill under the tongue (dry dose method), or dissolve a pill in a dropper bottle and administer this liquid (liquid method). Liquid dosing is considered gentler and less likely to worsen a cat's symptoms or to produce new symptoms. Whether using a dry or liquid dosing technique, make sure you never touch the remedy because this can render it ineffective.

How Is Homeopathy Used?

Two general categories of homeopathic treatment exist: acute and constitutional. The remedies mentioned in this book are for acute, or self-limiting, situations, such as puncture wounds, diarrhea, vomiting, or soreness from a fall. Characterized by their sudden onset, acute situations are short-lived, although they frequently require medical attention. This book doesn't cover constitutional treatments because they involve delving at a deeper level into a cat's mental and physical state. A person who has undergone a great deal of self-study can undertake constitutional treaments, but ideally, this is best left to a trained veterinary homeopath. To successfully use homeopathy calls for skill not only in choosing a homeopathic remedy but also in determining potency and dosage schedule.

Homeopathic remedies are pleasant-tasting and very well-suited for delicate animals like cats.

Homeopaths treat the individual cat, not the disease, so treatment that works for one cat won't necessarily be indicated for another, unless the two cats have the exact same set of symptoms. Homeopathic remedies are tailored to the cat's overall personality type because it's believed that each cat has a unique energy or "vital force" that manifests itself in ways unique to that cat—for instance, whether she's outgoing or shy, seeks or shuns warmth, and is or isn't restless.

Expect your first consultation with a homeopathic veterinarian to take an hour or more. That's because your veterinarian will ask detailed questions about your cat's overall personality, her likes and dislikes, her physical and mental symptoms, and what make the symptoms better or worse. Once the veterinary homeopath prescribes a remedy, you'll be asked to keep a record of any changes in your cat so the homeopath can evaluate the remedy choice and how well it works.

In many ways, homeopathy could be considered the perfect modality for cats. If used correctly, homeopathy is as safe and gentle for cats as it is for humans, and you don't need to worry about excretion by the liver or kidneys, or about toxicity in their fragile little bodies, as you would with regular drugs or herbs. Seeing homeopathy's fast, effective results can inspire awe. Fortunately, there's a renewed interest in homeopathy in the United States, so finding a veterinary homeopath should get easier with time. Homeopathy has never fallen into disfavor in Europe, India, South Africa, New Zealand, and Australia, so in these countries, homeopathy for pets—including cats—is considered a part of veterinary care.

If you are unable to purchase a *Repertory* or *Materia Media*, visit a website such as www.homeoint.org for free information.

Flower Essences

Flower essences are prepared by infusing flower petals at the peak of their bloom in spring water. A common preparation method is to soak petals in spring or artesian well water and place them in direct sunlight for around three hours. Sometimes the bowls are left out overnight to absorb energy from the moon and the stars. This infusion is believed to hold a plant's healing vibrational energy or life force. The essence of a plant is quite different, so plants that you'd otherwise avoid, such as red clover, you can safely use in essence form.

The English physician Edward Bach was instrumental in the development and use of flower remedy essences as we know them today. He developed thirty-eight flower remedies that he believed encompassed all possible mental conditions. Over the years, remedies or essences have been developed from various parts of the world from not just flowers, but also gems and other elements. It's believed that essences prepared from flowers in the area a person lives are more effective. Bach flower essences are the most well known and readily available, but feel free to experiment with other brands and varieties because they might more closely match your cat's energy. In other words, don't give up if you try a particular brand and don't see results, even after a certain length of time, such as a month.

How Do Flower Essences Work?

Flower essences are a gentle and effective way to help your cat deal with difficult situations, such as visits to the veterinarian, additions to the family, and other life changes. Flower essences work in subtle ways to undo negative influences, energy, or characteristics in a cat. In some cases, you'll notice the effect of flower essences within minutes. For instance, the Bach flower essence Rescue Remedy can help cats suffering from shock or trauma calm down very quickly. In most cases, however, flower essences elicit subtle changes over a period of time—usually a few weeks.

Flower essences are a gentle and safe way to help your cat deal with life's stresses.

Several books are available on the topic of flower essences, including more than one excellent repertory with detailed information for remedy selection. Chapter six contains recommendations of flower essences for behavioral issues.

How to Administer Flower Essences

You can use flower essences alone or in combination with one or more other flower essences. A popular technique is to prepare a stock bottle from one or more flower essences by filling a 1 ounce (28 ml) cobalt or dark brown dropper bottle with spring water. Then you can add two to three drops from the original flower essence bottle(s) into the dropper bottle. This stock bottle now has a diluted alcohol amount, and you can use it to administer flower essences to your cat.

Flower essences are usually preserved with brandy, so if you wish to avoid alcohol altogether, you can either use brands without alcohol or boil off the alcohol in one of the other brands. You can boil off the alcohol by adding a few drops of flower essences to a tablespoon or two of just-boiled water. Then you can add this mix to the stock bottle along with spring water to prepare a stock remedy bottle. The resulting mix will contain little or no alcohol and is safe for cats. If you plan to store this bottle for a long time, you can add one drop of brandy, vegetable glycerin, apple cider vinegar, or the Japanese herb red shiso.

You can use a dropper to administer flower essences orally or add to your cat's drinking water. You can also rub them on a cat's gums or apply them to exposed skin, such as on the paw pads, ears, and or nose. For acute situations, such as trauma, you might need only one or couple more doses. For chronic situations, your cat might need several doses before you see results. For the first few days, give your cat five or six equally spaced doses. Then taper off to three or four doses a day, and as you continue to see improvement, you can drop down to one or two doses. You can discontinue flower essences when your cat is back to her normal emotional state.

> Sometimes physical problems manifest as emotional problems, and vice versa. Giving your cat a flower essence for stress won't work if the stress stems from an unresolved physical problem.

General Guidelines for Minor Ailments

You can often handle scrapes, cuts, and other inevitable minor health problems at home with items from your kitchen or medicine cabinet. For such problems, home remedies work really well for cats, not only because you can easily administer them with quick results, but also because they help you avoid car rides and veterinarian visits—two things cat's aren't particularly fond of. Before administering a home remedy, call your veterinarian to make sure the problem is one you can treat at home. You can save your cat a lot of anguish by taking care of minor, nonlife-threatening problems at home. You can also sock away what you might have spent on emergency visits in a rainy-day fund to use for your cat when a real emergency occurs.

If your cat stays in your own front or backyard, make sure none of the plants are on the dangerous plants list.

Homeopathy for Acute Problems

Because acute ailments exhibit fairly typical symptoms, you can give homeopathic remedies for short-term relief. Homeopathy doesn't follow a strict dosing schedule, even for acute conditions, because each individual reacts differently to a remedy. The most conservative approach is to give one dose of a remedy, then wait and see. Give another dose only if you see some improvement in the original symptoms, and continue dosing only if there's still room for improvement in her symptoms. If her symptoms change, discontinue the remedy because it no longer matches her symptoms, and she may need a different remedy. Use these general guidelines for homeopathy:

- Don't touch the remedy; if a pellet drops on the floor, discard it.
- Don't give it with food or liquids. Give it at least thirty minutes before or after feeding.

- Store all remedies in a cool, dry place and away from strong odors and light.
- Give your cat only one remedy at any given time.
- Stick to lower potencies, such as 6X, 6C, 12X, 12C, 30X, and 30C.
- If the problem resolves, stop giving the remedy. Also, don't continue to give it if you don't see a positive change after two or three doses.
- Don't give your cat any homeopathic remedy long term without the advice of a veterinarian trained in homeopathy.
- Don't use combination remedies such as those labeled "diarrhea" or "itching," which contain several remedies—as many as fifteen, in some cases.
- Ideally, don't mix homeopathic remedies with herbs and other supplements.

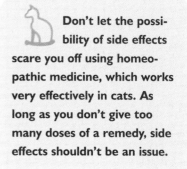

Don't let the possibility of side effects scare you off using homeopathic medicine, which works very effectively in cats. As long as you don't give too many doses of a remedy, side effects shouldn't be an issue.

If you have difficulty administering remedies from a dropper, you can dissolve two or three pellets in a small glass saucer of milk for your cat to lap up. Many cats can't tolerate milk, but if your cat likes and tolerates cow's milk, it's perfectly safe to give it to her. If your cat is lactose-intolerant, you can instead dissolve the pellets in goat's milk, which cats tolerate more readily. Just one or two licks of this liquid are enough for the remedy to work.

Liquid Dosing Technique

Liquid dosing is a gentle way to administer homeopathic remedies. Keep in mind, however, that too many doses of the same potency of a remedy can cause problems, including worsening of symptoms or the appearance of new symptoms. To avoid problems, don't use the same potency more than a few times at most.

To prepare a dosage bottle, dissolve one pill or pellet in a sterilized dark-colored bottle that holds 1 to 4 ounces (28 to 120 ml). Fill the dropper bottle the rest of the way with spring or distilled water. Squirt as much of a full dropper's contents as you can into your cat's mouth.

If you don't have a bottle, dissolve a pellet or two in a saucer or glass. To administer, use a drinking straw. If you need to give more than three or four doses, you'll need to dilute the liquid with each successive dose.

A simple technique is to use one spoonful of the water from the original bottle or glass and stir it into a clean glass containing another 1 to 4 ounces (28 to 120 ml) of water. Gently stir the water in the second glass about ten times and, using a straw, give your cat a spoonful of the liquid from the second glass.

If you're using a dropper bottle, after diluting, strike the bottle against a book or the palm of your hand to energize it. Dilute and shake after every set of four to five doses because this changes the remedy's potency and energy.

A Quick and Easy Slippery Elm Bark Mixture

Slippery elm bark is a soothing herb excellent for treating tummy upsets, nausea, and urinary problems. You can find powdered slippery elm bark in the bulk food section of some grocery and health food stores.

INGREDIENTS AND SUPPLIES

$1/2$ teaspoon (2.5 g) slippery elm bark powder from capsules or $1/4$ teaspoon (1.2 g) slippery elm bark bulk powder (powder from the bulk food section is thicker and denser, so it takes half as much to get the same results as the powder contained in capsules)

2 tbsp (28 ml) boiled water

small glass jar with a lid

INSTRUCTIONS

Pour $1/4$ teaspoon (1.2 g) of powdered slippery elm bark or the entire contents of two size 0 capsules of 350 to 400 mg slippery elm bark into a clean, empty glass jar such as a baby food jar. Then pour 2 tbsp (28 ml) of just-boiled water into this jar. Mix gently, and fasten the lid until it's almost completely tight but not all the way. After half an hour, completely close the lid on the jar and shake. By this time, the mixture should be cool enough to use.

DOSAGE

Give your cat 3 to 5 cc two to three times a day with a plastic syringe or dropper. Make sure there's at least thirty minutes to an hour between the administration of slippery elm bark and any other meal or other medication.

Bites and Stings

You should consult a veterinarian if you have any doubts about a bite or sting, but there are some gentle ways to give your cat relief from a superficial bite or sting. Since cats groom themselves so meticulously, make sure that everything you apply for cuts, bruises, and stings is safe to ingest because it's likely to end up in their stomachs. That's why we've taken so much care to ensure that you can safely use anything recommended, not only this chapter, but in this entire book.

If your cat has a superficial bite or sting, you can take the following steps. First, clean the area with warm water. Then you can use a cotton ball to dab one of the following on the affected area:

- a paste of baking soda and water
- a solution of $^1/_2$ teaspoon (2.5 g) Epsom salt in $^1/_2$ cup (120 ml) of warm water
- emu oil with no added ingredients
- organic apple cider vinegar

If swelling and itching accompany the sting, you can give your cat the homeopathic remedy *Apis* internally.

Cuts and Bruises

Because cats have such sharp claws, they sometimes inflict puncture wounds on each other during rough play. Their claws can inflict some rather deep cuts into the skin, trapping bacteria underneath. When this happens, first snip the fur around the wound and apply a warm compress or wash thoroughly with mild soap and water. Then, depending on whether you feel home care is appropriate, try one of the choices laid out in this section.

HERBAL REMEDIES

Stevia is a South American herb that has superb healing properties. It works extremely well on small, superficial cuts to stop bleeding and promote healing. You can use either apply the extract form directly on the cut or dissolve some stevia powder into colloidal silver, green myrtle hydrosol, or just plain water and then use some gauze to dab it on the cut. Alternatively, you can apply echinacea and goldenseal powder or herbal tincture or a mix of both both to the cut.

HOMEOPATHIC REMEDIES

You can use calendula and hypericum tinctures either alone or together to treat wounds; don't substitute the equivalent herbal extracts because they don't have the same effects. Only use calendula if there's no sign of infection because it can seal the wound quickly, which would trap infection inside. Hypericum is a safer choice for wounds and cuts, especially in areas rich in nerves, such as paw pads.

- bromelain, an enzyme found in the pineapple plant, can be given twice a day for a total daily dose of 500 mg along with a maximum of 100 mg per day of turmeric capsules or turmeric powder mixed in food.

SUPPLEMENTS THAT HELP WITH INFLAMMATION FROM BITES, CUTS, OR WOUNDS

These remedies work for wounds and bruises.

- aconite: first remedy given following a wound

- apis: for red, swollen puncture wounds

- arnica: excellent for bruises; also helps with accompanying trauma

- hypericum: for bruising or injury that affects the nerves

- ledum: for deep puncture wounds, such as those caused by splinters and thorns

- pyrogenium: for swollen and infected wounds that emit a foul odor

- silica: particularly useful for splinters with thin, watery pus

- staphysagria: for pain from deep cuts, including surgical incisions

- symphytum: for wounds that penetrate to and involve bone

- urtica or cantharis: for burns

Did You Know?

Hairballs are indigestible protein, made up of 15 to 30 percent fat. Enzymes can't penetrate the coating around hairballs to have much effect on them. Most over-the-counter hairball products grease the intestinal tract, but do little else. Lecithin works as an emulsifier, fighting the fat in hairballs with fat to break them up. If your cat has a hairball problem, add a small amount of fiber to his diet and lecithin from egg yolks, not from soy. Fiber and egg yolk lecithin also work well to prevent hairballs from forming.

Pre- and Postsurgery Care

The night before surgery, you can administer one dose of arnica 30C. The morning of the surgery, give your cat a dose of arnica just before surgery. As soon as can see your cat following the surgery, give her another dose of arnica 30C.

If your cat doesn't seem to be recovering from anesthesia or seems disoriented, give her one dose of phosphorus 30C. If your cat not only seems disoriented and confused but also seems to be in shock or suffering from trauma, give her a dose of aconite 30C instead of phosphorous.

If your cat seems to be in pain, staphysagria 30C may help. Don't exceed three doses, and if it doesn't bring about relief, reassess the situation. Call your veterinarian if your cat isn't better within twenty-four hours because she might need a painkiller or need to be seen by her veterinarian.

You can follow the same protocol for dental surgery with one change. If your cat has trouble eating after dental extractions, you can alternate hypericum 30C with arnica 30C.

You can use a combination flower essence or remedy sold under such names as Rescue Remedy, Calming Essence, or Quaking Grass at any time before or after the surgery. It will help your cat deal with the fear, anxiety, and trauma associated with surgical procedures.

Parasites

A parasite is an organism that lives on or in a host and obtains its nutrients from the host. It can cause such problems as anemia from blood loss, skin allergies and inflammation, and digestive upset. Cats can pick up internal pests, such as worms, and external ones, such as fleas, lice, and ear mites. A strong immune system is a cat's best defense against parasites and disease. A species-appropriate diet goes a long way toward achieving this. Cats or kittens rescued from less-than-ideal situations often have parasites. Some anecdotal evidence suggests that you can prevent parasites by administering a

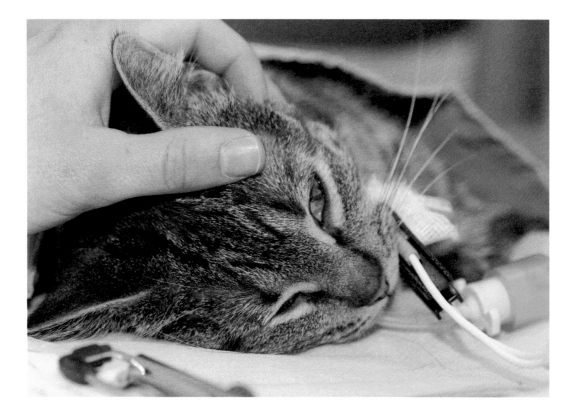

$^1/_4$ teaspoon (1.2 ml) of unfiltered apple cider vinegar in 4 ounces (120 ml) of water. Apple cider vinegar is tart, so you'd most likely have to do this using a plastic syringe because your cats in all likelihood wouldn't be too thrilled to have apple cider vinegar mixed into their food.

Gentle methods will help your cat heal faster, so anything you can do in this regard will be good for your cat.

Be very careful with parasite medications sold over the counter at grocery and pet supply stores; several have caused very serious harm to cats, even death in some cases. Have your veterinarian make a definitive diagnosis, and use prescribed medication because, in the long run, it may not only be the safest but the most cost-effective option as well.

Health Issues in Newly Adopted Cats

Stray cats or cats adopted from an outside colony of strays tend to have very different health issues than other cats. Outside cats tend to be more prone to parasites and worms. Indoor cats are sometimes exposed to upper respiratory illnesses that can spread easily, adversely affecting cats with compromised immune systems.

Have any cats that have been living outside thoroughly checked out for parasites and worms. Tapeworms use fleas as a carrier, so if your cat has fleas, she might also have tapeworms. Tapeworms look like bits of rice; you can see these segments with the naked eye either in your cat's stool or just under her tail. You can also sometimes see roundworms with the naked eye. Other worms, such as whipworms and hookworms, can only be detected in a stool sample using a microscope. Having a stool sample examined is also an easy way to determine if your new cat or kitten has protozoal parasites, such as Giardia or Coccidia.

Use the garlic-infused olive oil mix (page 27) to smother ear mites. Using an eyedropper or cotton ball, apply this oil every day for a week to kill mites, then three to four times a week for at least six weeks to kill larvae and prevent recurrence. You can also add the herbs mullein and yellow dock (Rumex crispus) in tincture form to this mix (four drops of each tincture to twenty drops of water) because they have a long tradition of use in Europe for skin problems such as eruptions, itching, sores, and infections. If the ear mite infestation is too severe, seek veterinary treatment.

Ticks

Cats can acquire Lyme disease if bitten by a deer tick that's not removed within twenty-four hours—ideally, within eight to ten hours. Cats can't get Lyme disease from animals or humans, nor can they transmit it to others.

Flea collars don't repel ticks, so if you let your cats go outside, check them over thoroughly for red, inflamed areas when they come back into the house.

If a tick buries under your cat's skin, don't apply a smothering lubricant, such as petroleum jelly. That will cause the tick to release neurotoxins into your cat's skin. If you spot a tick, use a pair of tweezers to remove it as close to the head as possible. If a tick buries under your cat's skin and you don't extract the entire tick, enough of its mouth might be left behind to continue to infect your cat.

Use a firm twisting motion to remove all of the tick. Avoid jerking on the tick's body, Once removed, apply colloidal silver liberally to the area. You can use any concentration up to 500 ppm.

HOW DO I KNOW IF MY CAT HAS CONTRACTED LYME DISEASE?

To determine if your cat has Lyme disease, have your veterinarian run a blood test for titers or antibodies to *Borrelia* bacteria. Western blot is the most definitive test because the ELISA test often gives a false-negative result.

External symptoms of Lyme disease can begin within a few hours but sometimes don't show up for five to ten days following a bite. They can include:

- depression or lethargy

- limping or lameness; shifting from one leg to the other and moving from the back to the front of the body

- loss of appetite or poor appetite

- low-grade fever

- swollen joints or lymph glands

HOW IS LYME DISEASE TREATED?

If you suspect your cat was exposed, you can give her a single dose of homeopathic Ledum 1M in liquid dose. The only other proven effective treatments are the antibiotics amoxicillin and doxycycline. Yogurt inhibits both these antibiotics, so this is one case in which you should give a probiotic pill, not yogurt, during the course of antibiotics.

If you can remove a tick and you think your cat may be infected, save the tick in a jar and ask your veterinarian to send it to a laboratory to be analyzed for *Borrelia* bacteria.

Worms

The most common types of worms are roundworms, whipworms, tapeworms, hookworms, and flukes. Don't attempt to diagnose the type of worm your cat has and take a chance on administering the wrong remedy. Instead, let your veterinarian examine your cat's stool sample to determine the treatment course and how to prevent reinfestation.

As already mentioned, you can see some worms—such as tapeworm, which resemble bits of rice—in your cat's feces and in the hair or on the skin around her anus. Others can only be seen under a microscope. It's a good idea to have your veterinarian periodically test your cat's feces for worms.

One challenge in treating worms is that most of the herbs used to expel worms, such as wormwood (*Artemisia absinthium*), are quite harsh; they have to be strong enough to kill the parasite but not harm the cat. Garlic, for example, is safe for humans but you can't give it to cats, and several herbal parasite formulas contain garlic, along with other possibly harmful herbs.

In cases of moderate to severe infestations, your best bet is to use a drug from your veterinarian. Your cat will need only one pill or a very short course of treatment to take care of the problem. With herbs, you face a compliance issue because the herbs used to kill parasites taste awful, so your cats won't accept them in their food. You can pill them with herbal capsules, but herbs still take a lot longer to act than drugs; during the time the herbs are slowly killing the parasites, the parasites can still cause damage to your cat by sucking on her blood and draining vital nutrients. Keep this in mind when you read the home-remedies section.

Home Remedies for Worms

You can use the following remedies used alone or combined for maximum effectiveness. You can mix them in to your cat's food each day for at least three to four weeks.

- 1 teaspoon (5 g) ground pumpkin seeds and ¹/₂ to 1 teaspoon (2.5 to 5 g) pureed or pulped carrots added to each meal is particularly effective for tapeworms and cleansing the intestinal tract. If you can, get wild black carrots because they work better than run-of-the-mill carrots from the supermarket.

- The digestive enzymes papain, bromelain, amylase, lipase, and cellulose are useful. You can also give these in capsule form.

- ¹/₄ teaspoon (1.2 g) of food-grade diatomaceous earth powder works on all types of worms as well as fleas. Make certain you don't get pool-grade diatomaceous earth; also, it's very fine and powdery and can be dangerous when inhaled, so don't let it get into your or your cat's lungs.

You can dose your cat with one capsule per day of one of these all-purpose worming herbs for short-term use—a maximum of six weeks. However, because they're so powerful, only give them if approved by your cat's veterinarian.

- bitter melon or gourd, or karela (*Momordica charantia*); keep in mind that this also has glucose-lowering capabilities—an important consideration for diabetic cats

- cloves (*Eugenia caryophyllata*)

- neem (*Azadirachta indica*)

- southernwood (*Artemisia abrotanum*)

Normal Vital Signs

A cat's normal temperature ranges from 100°F to 102.5°F (37.8°C to 39.2°C).

A cat's normal pulse is sixty to one hundred and forty beats per minute.

HOW TO CHECK A CAT'S VITAL SIGNS:

- **Heartbeat:** Place a finger on the inside of the thigh near the groin and feel gently for a pulse from the artery. Use a watch with a second hand and, for one minute, count the number of heartbeats. Another place you can check a cat's heartbeat is just behind the left armpit, between the third and sixth ribs.

- **Temperature:** Even though a child's ear thermometer has been shown to consistently record a slightly lower temperature than a regular thermometer, one of its main virtues is that you can use it more easily on an uncooperative cat. For a more accurate reading, you can use a quick-reading digital thermometer. Reset the temperature setting, apply some petroleum jelly on the thermometer, and insert it about an inch (2.5 cm) into your cat's anus; hold it there until the thermometer beeps.

Of the above, try neem on its own first before you bring out the stronger, more bitter ones listed. You can also rub neem externally to treat lice or add it to a gentle shampoo.

Fleas

A healthy diet should, in theory, make a cat's body unattractive to fleas. However, anyone who has lived in a humid climate knows all too well that fleas are tenacious and can prey on even the best cared-for and fed cats. Fleas spend the majority of their time in your home and yard, not on your cat, so treating your cat isn't enough; you'll need to deal with all the places fleas live.

Many reasons exist for aggressive treatment of a flea infestation. Fleas can cause severe allergies in cats. In some cases, a single fleabite can cause allergic dermatitis in a cat. Fleas also cause blood loss, which can lead to anemia. And fleas are the vector for tapeworm, so a cat with fleas is also vulnerable to tapeworm. Unless you deal with the entire flea problem, killing existing tapeworms won't be enough because the problem will just recur.

HOW TO RID YOUR HOME AND YOUR CATS OF FLEAS

- **Yards:** Spread beneficial worms, known as nematodes, liberally all over the outside areas of your home. You can buy nematodes at your local garden supply or hardware store. Certain plants repel fleas, so you can plant them outside, but many, such as pennyroyal, are harmful for cats. So don't plant these if your or any neighborhood cats frequent your yard.

- **Cat:** Bathe your cat in a mild shampoo. Allow five to ten minutes for the shampoo to soak in and smother the fleas. After a bath, use a fine-tooth flea comb to capture any remaining fleas and drop them into the sink or in a container of soapy water. Although essential oils are dangerous for cats, you can rub a mix of one part lavender hydrosol, one part lemon verbena hydrosol, and two parts spring water into your cat's fur a few times a day. You can also spray this mix on your cat's bedding and on any upholstery in the house.

- **Home:** You can prepare the recipe below, using ingredients mostly found in your grocery store, to make a very effective flea-powder mix that will rid your home of fleas. Diatomaceous earth is the only product you'll need to buy in a specialty store.

Flea-Powder Mix

Feel free to experiment and change the proportions based on availability in your area:

INGREDIENTS

50 percent borax powder

25 percent food-grade diatomaceous earth*

15 percent dried lavender herb run through coffee or spice grinder

5 percent cornstarch

5 percent baking soda

INSTRUCTIONS

Combine all the ingredients and then rub the prepared mix into the carpets and upholstery in your home. Let this powdered mixture sit overnight or up to twenty-four hours if possible. Vacuum thoroughly. You might need to do this every week if you're dealing with a heavy infestation. Otherwise, doing this every two weeks or even once a month during the hot, humid months should take care of the problem.

* Diatomaceous earth can cause extreme lung irritation as well as silicosis. Handle the powder carefully, and don't let any fly around. Most importantly, for their own safety, keep your cat and your family members away from any areas being treated. Protect yourself by wearing a mask while handling diatomaceous earth so you don't inhale any of the powder.

Digestive Upset

Vomiting or diarrhea can dehydrate a cat, so make sure you give your cat plenty of liquids, such as plain water or chicken broth when they're sick (see the recipe on page 73). Cats suffering from constipation also need more water in their systems. If your cat won't drink on her own, give her liquids by mouth with a plastic syringe; if necessary, she may need to receive subcutaneous fluids under a veterinarian's supervision.

Some cats do well with both soluble fiber, such as psyllium, and insoluble fiber, such as wheat bran; others can tolerate only one or neither. So use a cautious approach by starting slowly and building up. Soluble fiber typically helps more with diarrhea and insoluble fiber with constipation, but your cat's system may in general accept one better than the other.

If your cat has one of the following sets of symptoms, don't attempt treatment at home:

■ both vomiting and diarrhea

■ either vomiting or diarrhea for more than twenty-four hours

■ blood in the vomit (this will look like coffee grounds)

■ lethargy between bouts of vomiting

■ pain, bloating, and tenderness in the abdominal region

■ vomiting with fever over 101°F (38°C)

■ rapid breathing or pulse rate

■ blood in the stool or tarry, black stool

■ scooting behavior or a swollen anal area

- excessive drooling
- vomiting shortly after eating

Vomiting

Cats hardly ever vomit unless something is wrong. A certain food could lead to an isolated vomiting episode, but vomiting could also indicate a more serious underlying digestive problem. It could also be a symptom of infection, heartworms, and even cancer.

If your cat ever has a vomiting episode, note the frequency and color of vomit, how soon after eating it occurs, and whether there's undigested food in the vomit. Such information can help if you should you need to give a homeopathic remedy for palliative relief until the veterinarian can see your cat.

HOMEOPATHY

These homeopathic treatments may help:

- arsenicum 30: for violent, very frequent vomiting made worse by drinking cold water or eating

- ipecac 30: for nausea with vomiting that provides no relief (cat looks miserable after throwing up)

- nux vomica 30: for violent, ineffectual retching that doesn't lead to vomiting

Diarrhea

Rich food as well as sudden changes in food can contribute to diarrhea. Should this occur, give your cat homemade chicken broth (see page 73) with acidophilus and digestive enzymes

When to Seek Immediate Veterinary Care

PHYSICAL CHANGES

Watch your cat so that you know what she's like when she's healthy. That way, you're more likely to notice any deviations from the norm and you can take appropriate action. If your cat is an enthusiastic eater, for instance, you'll recognize a sudden decrease in appetite as a warning sign.

BEHAVIORAL CHANGES

Deviations from normal behavior for your cat might signal either a physical or mental problem. An outgoing, active, playful cat who suddenly becomes withdrawn, starts to sleep a lot, or loses interest in running and playing could be letting you know she has a problem. Or such behavior might signal sadness or depression—for instance, following the passing of a family member. Ingestion of poisonous plants or a hazardous chemical such as antifreeze could also result in your cat becoming quiet and withdrawn.

added to it. However, if you see no improvement in a day or so, take your cat to the veterinarian's office because your cat may have lost electrolytes. Don't use over-the-counter antidiarrheals because they contain bismuth and salicylates, both harmful to cats.

Diarrhea can also result from more serious problems, such as parasites, bacteria, ingestion of foreign material, IBD, pancreatitis, liver disease, distemper, and cancer. As with vomiting, keep a close eye on your cat, and note the color of the stool and whether it contains mucous or blood.

These can help a cat with diarrhea:

- 3 to 5 cc of slippery elm syrup (see page 128), best given thirty to sixty minutes before or after a meal

- $^1/_{16}$ teaspoon (0.3 g) wheat bran mixed in food

- $^1/_8$ teaspoon (0.6 g) psyllium husk seed or $^1/_8$ teaspoon (0.6 g) acacia gum mixed with 2 tablespoons of warm water

- $^1/_{16}$ teaspoon (0.3 g) unfiltered pure apple cider vinegar mixed with 2 teaspoons (10 ml) water

- tea brewed from bags or loose, dried chamomile flowers or blackberry leaves

- Charcoal capsules help absorb toxins but shouldn't be used long-term

HOMEOPATHIC REMEDIES

- Aloe socotrina: for stool with mucous

- Arsenicum album: for food poisoning–type symptoms; for instance, if your cat eats meat that may have been a bit "off," this would be a good remedy; symptoms include restlessness and anxiety

- Podophyllum: for profuse diarrhea with offensive smell and gas

- Pulsatilla: for yellow stool, particularly if consistency changes from stool to stool and cat complains

- Veratrum album: for diarrhea accompanied by projectile vomiting

Constipation

Cats on a raw diet tend to produce smaller stools, and frequency will vary (based on the cat) from once a day to every other day. Because a raw diet is high in moisture and fiber from meat and vegetables, cats on a natural raw diet are less likely to suffer from either constipation or diarrhea. However, some cats are prone to chronic constipation. Keep a watchful eye for straining, and at the first sign of any blood in the stool or any protrusion or fissures, take your cat to her veterinarian immediately.

If, however, your cat has an occasional bout of constipation, you can take some steps at home to provide some relief. Never give your cat an enema product meant for humans; these contains sodium phosphate, which can be fatal to cats.

HOMEOPATHIC REMEDIES

- Bryonia: give this if your cat is listless, thirsty, irritable, and produces dry hard stools

- Carbo veg: you can give this if your cat is suffering from indigestion after eating a rich meal; it's good for gas and general indigestion issues

- Graphites: give this if your cat has alternating diarrhea and constipation symptoms.

- Nux vomica: this helps with ineffectual straining with irritability

- Plumbum: give this if your cat has hard, black stools

Is There a Natural Antibiotic?

For a minor infection, you can use one or all of these together on a short-term basis, along with probiotics.

- **Colloidal silver: You can give 50 ppm or less internally, and 100 to 500 ppm externally.**

- **Grapefruit seed extract: Give one pill a day; the liquid version is challenging to administer internally because it's extremely bitter. You can mix one drop into a pound of your cat's raw mix if you want to administer the liquid version. Never use grapefruit seed extract liquid undiluted topically because it can burn a cat's skin.**

- **Olive leaf extract: You can give one capsule per day mixed with food.**

- raphanus: this can help if your cat has constipation with no attempts to use the litter box, with or without painful gas

- silica: use this if your cat attempts to go but has trouble defecating

With the exception of slippery elm bark, where you should allow a thirty- to sixty-minute gap between the giving the medicine and any meals, you can give your cat these supplements alone or added to food.

- 1 teaspoon (5 ml) aloe vera juice; make sure the brand has no sodium benzoate, canageenan, or potassium sorbate

- 1/4 to 1/2 (1.2 to 2.5 ml) teaspoon canned pure pumpkin

- 1/8 teaspoon (0.6 g) cold-pressed grape seed oil or extra virgin olive oil

- 1/8 teaspoon (0.6 g) ghee or unsalted butter

- 1/8 teaspoon (0.6 g) wheat bran, with or without a fat source

- 1/8 teaspoon (0.6 ml) psyllium husk seed mixed with two tablespoons (28 ml) warm water

- 3 to 5 cc slippery elm broth (see page 126)

Litter Box Issues

Although it's more challenging to do this in multicat households, it's very useful to keep a close eye on all your cats' litter box habits, including frequency and appearance, so you can discover deviations from the norm.

Straining in the Litter Box

If your cat jumps in and out of the litter box frequently and appears to have trouble urinating, she needs immediate veterinary attention because she could be blocked. This condition can be fatal, so play it safe and get your cat medical attention as soon as possible.

Frequent or Increased Urination

Several serious diseases, such as diabetes and kidney insufficiency or failure, as well as UTIs, cause frequent or increased urination. If your cat is suddenly making too many trips to the litter box, take a urine sample along with your cat to the veterinarian. The only way to get a clean urine sample at home is to catch it midstream with a saucer or long-handled spoon placed under your cat while she's in her litter box.

If your cat looks affronted when you attempt to catch her urine midstream, you can settle for a nonsterile sample (see page 146). This will still allow your veterinarian to test for the urine's specific gravity and glucose, among other things. Your veterinarian will also be able to determine how well your cat is concentrating her urine and test for the presence of crystals, protein, and glucose in the urine.

Prolapse

A cat that strains in the litter box during defecation may occasionally develop a prolapse, which is the protrusion of anal or rectal tissue. If this happens, watch to make sure the tissue goes back in place within a few hours; if it doesn't, take your cat to the veterinarian because this tissue can become necrotic, which would be fatal to your cat. Bright red blood in the stool accompanied by prolapse is a sign of bleeding in the lower gastrointestinal tract; black, tarry stool is a sign of bleeding higher up in the GI tract. Bleeding signals irritation, so take your cat to the veterinarian if this happens.

> **Apply sesame oil to your cat's nose if she suffers from dryness or sniffles.**

To help prevent the recurrence of prolapse, take steps to ensure your cat gets enough fiber in her diet. One way to do this is with pumpkin and psyllium husk (if your cat can tolerate it) mixed with water. Homeopathic treatment with a veterinarian trained in this field is a gentle way to deal with this rather serious problem.

How to Obtain a Nonsterile Urine Sample

If your cat will use an empty litter box, this will work best because you can simply suck the urine into a plastic syringe, which you can then take to your veterinarian. Or you can pour the urine into a sterile glass or plastic container, such as an empty baby food jar. You can refrigerate this sample for up to twelve hours.

However, a lot of cats won't use an empty litter box. In such a case, let your cat pick from a litter box that contains one of the following, nonabsorbent (except for paper towels) items:

- **no litter but lined with paper towels**
- **no litter but filled with strips of parchment or wax paper**
- **no litter but a long roll of parchment paper lining the pan**
- **her regular litter or no litter with a large plastic trash bag laid on top; if your cat is a digger, she might attempt to use the litter under the bag, so first try this without any litter in the box**
- **special gravel-like litter, available from your veterinarian**
- **clean aquarium gravel or any small, pea-size gravel or rocks without sharp edges**
- **packing peanuts**

If you use paper towels, wring them out fairly quickly or else you might not have a large enough sample—approximately 3 to 5 ml—for the veterinarian to test.

Appetite and Weight Loss

Both increases and decreases in appetite can signal problems. When you pet your cat each day, feel for her ribs, and take note of whether she has gained or lost weight. Healthy cats should maintain their weight, and appetite shouldn't vary greatly from one day to the next. It's a good idea to monitor your cat's weight periodically by using a baby scale or weighing yourself holding her and then subtracting from this your weight alone.

Increased Appetite

A particularly worrisome symptom in an older cat, increased appetite can signal a serious disease, such as an overactive thyroid gland or diabetes. If constant hunger is accompanied with weight loss despite an increase in food intake, suspect hyperthyroidism and get blood tests done, particularly a free T4 test, at your veterinarian's office. A high number on the T4 test indicates an overactive thyroid.

Sudden Weight Loss

If your cat has sudden weight loss with no change in diet, it could be from inadequate protein in her diet leading to muscle wasting. Sudden weight loss warrants immediate attention from a veterinarian.

Holistic Supply Kit Checklist

This list of herbs, supplements, and homeopathic remedies contains some must-haves and reliable standbys you will find yourself reaching for quite frequently. In addition, always keep some chicken broth in the freezer, as well as a fail-safe food your cat will eat if sick, such as meat baby food or prescription canned food.

HERBS AND SUPPLEMENTS

Psyllium husk—can be added along with water to food in case of upset stomach or constipation

Slippery elm bark powder—for vomiting, diarrhea, constipation, and nausea.

Digestive enzymes and probiotics—useful for digestive upset

Stinging nettles—use upon first signs of sneezing

Lysine—for herpes flare-ups, including sneezing and watery eyes

Colloidal silver (CS)—for topical use, either neat or diluted in eyes, ears, and nose

Turmeric—mixed with coconut butter or CS for topical use on skin conditions such as itching and superficial wounds

Echinacea—apply directly on wounds to prevent infection and promote healing

Rescue Remedy or other flower essence combination—for shock, trauma, and terror

HOMEOPATHIC REMEDIES

Aconite—give at the first sign of a respiratory problem

Ledum—use when your cat gets bitten by any animal or insect

Arnica—useful for any situation where your cat is in distress; can be used along with Rescue Remedy

Urtica urens tincture—use in diluted form externally for burns, rashes, and skin irritation and internally to promote the flow of urine until you can get medical attention

Hopefully, your cat will never need any of the home care outlined in this chapter, but keep a kit containing these remedies on hand should she ever encounter any of these problems. The most important thing to keep in mind when treating cats' health problems is that what works for humans and other species won't always have the same benefits for cats. This doesn't mean we should abandon alternative modalities; rather, we need to approach them with a cat's unique physiology in mind.

CHAPTER SIX

Understanding Cat Behavior

"Cats don't like change without their consent."

ROGER A. CARAS

Cats behave in ways that are often mysterious to the humans in their lives. However, understanding cat behavior is the first step toward dealing with any issue in a humane manner. Keep two simple rules in mind when attempting to curb your cat of a bad habit: first, know that your cat isn't being mean or spiteful and second, never hit or scream at a cat because your cat will associate the punishment with you rather than the act. Your cat will immediately understand and appreciate praise and encouragement, which work well as positive reinforcements for your cat's actions.

This chapter covers the following common behavioral issues:

- jumping on counters, stoves, and other forbidden areas of the house

- scratching carpets

- biting and acting aggressively toward humans and the other animals in the house

- waking up humans early in the morning to get attention and possibly food

- soiling, spraying, and other issues of elimination outside the litter box

You can address all these issues without resorting to drugs, getting rid of your cat, or inflicting cruel and painful procedures such as declawing. A multi-pronged plan that involves behavior modification on the human's part, redirection for the cat, use of gentle remedies such as flower essences, and rewards for good feline behavior works the best.

Rule Out Physical Problems

Your cat may display new behavior problems as a symptom of a physical ailment. In this chapter, we're assuming that you and your veterinarian have ruled out physical problems and the problem is behavioral. For example, if a cat who's good about using his litter box suddenly stops using it, it could be his way of communicating he has a medical problem such as a UTI that needs attention. When you've dealt with the core problem, the aberrant behavior usually goes away.

Think Like a Cat

These creatures of habit settle into familiar routines very quickly. Major life changes, such as the addition of a new human or animal to the household or a move to a new house, can understandably cause stress. In each situation, imagine yourself in your cat's place, and evaluate whether your cat's behavior is reasonable, given his perception of the circumstances. For example, although a human baby is a great source of joy for the parents, to a cat the infant is a noisy newcomer who takes attention away from him. Areas of the house previously available to your cat are suddenly inaccessible, and humans who doted on him no longer have as much time for him. Feelings of abandonment are only natural under these circumstances. If a human child can feel this way about a new sibling, why not a cat? Think of how you would feel if changes took place around you and you didn't understand the reason, extent, and possible permanence of these changes and you'll begin to understand what might be going on inside your cat's head. His reactions are perfectly normal given his position in the household.

Flower Essences for Mental Health

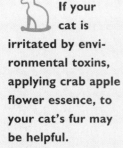

If your cat is irritated by environmental toxins, applying crab apple flower essence, to your cat's fur may be helpful.

Sometimes a cat with an unresolved physical problem or one dealing with a terminal illness will exhibit mental symptoms. Flower essences are a noninvasive way to help your cats deal with their emotional issues. The following table lists gentle, effective options for various maladies that plague cats.

You can use essences alone or in combinations of up to five at any given time. Allow three to four weeks to determine if they have been effective. Prepare a remedy bottle by adding two drops of each essence into a 1-ounce (28 ml) dark dropper bottle. Administer a dropperful several times a day by adding it to your cats' drinking water, by mouth, or by dabbing it on their paws, ears, and other exposed areas of their body.

Common Behavioral Concerns	Flower Essences
Grief, sadness, and depression, including from loss of a beloved companion	Bleeding heart, honeysuckle, sweet chestnut, gorse
Despondency or gloom not limited to illness	Borage, elm, gentian, mustard, penstemon
Stress, which can show up as fur-pulling or over-grooming	Cherry plum
Nervous, jittery, or shy behavior	Mimulus
Vague or equivocal fears	Aspen
Aggression, dominance, and hostility, with or without biting	Snapdragon, tiger lily, vine
Under-confident, possibly clingy and needy behavior	Chicory
Issues, such as adjustment of new cat or kitten	Walnut
Acting as if at wit's end or at limit of tolerance	Sweet chestnut
Fighting	Beech, walnut
Tense, hyperactive behavior	Vervain, chamomile
Behavior in response to change	Cosmo, quaking grass
Aggression from feelings of paranoia and mistrust, perhaps from earlier abuse	Oregon grape
Trauma, hysteria	Red clover, Rescue Remedy, quaking grass
Spraying	Willow, agrimony
Mistrust	Baby blue eyes
Intolerance	Beech, willow, yellow star tulip
Sudden need to be left alone	Water violet
Fear (in the case of feral or cats with limited human interaction)	Aspen, red clover
Jealousy for existing cats	Holly, impatiens, chicory
High-strung behavior	Impatiens, lavender, chamomile
Terror	Rock rose, Rescue Remedy, quaking grass
Timidity (including for a cat that's being picked on)	Larch, centaury, heather, sunflower

Should You Let Your Cats Outside?

Some cats rescued from the outdoors simply won't stay inside, despite your best efforts. In this case, your cat probably won't be persuaded to stay indoors, but here are some good reasons to try.

- Cats don't do well in areas where there's a lot of traffic because they don't have the road sense to survive in those situations.

- Depending on where you live, your cat could be exposed to infectious diseases, such as FeLV, FIV, FIP, and rabies.

- Cats can suffer injury or death from poisoning or attacks by humans and other predators.

- Cats, particularly males even when neutered, are prone to fights with other cats outside. When they come back in the house, they might bring some of this behavior into their home environment. For instance, they're likely to continue spraying inside the house if they do this when outside.

- An inside cat has a much longer lifespan and one free from the stresses and dangers of the outside world.

Although outside cats get a lot of stimulation—perhaps too much—inside cats can also be active if their caregivers pay attention to their needs. Toys, interactive or otherwise, are a great way for cats to simulate outside activities such as those related to hunting—stalking, pouncing, and attacking. Playing will provide your cats the exercise they need to stay healthy as well as the mental stimulation of being involved in something other than eating and sleeping, so they're less likely to seek inappropriate outlets for their energy.

Bringing Home a New Baby

Parents-to-be can use several strategies, even before the baby's birth, to get their cats used to the changes that will occur in the household. One is to give the cats a little less attention a few weeks before the child's birth. During this time, limit access to any areas where the cat won't be allowed once the baby arrives so that your cat can get used to off-limit areas. You can also play recordings of gurgling, crying, and other baby sounds to help your cat get used to these sounds. Let your cat sniff the baby's clothing and furniture as you get the nursery ready so your cat feels more involved.

While your baby is still at the hospital, bring her blanket home so your cats can get used to the new baby smell and not view her as foreign. When the baby arrives, while holding her, let the cats sniff her so that they can satisfy their curiosity. Let your cats be around during diaper changes and other activities that involve your new baby, and include them in conversations so they still feel a part of the family. Squeeze in as much play time with your cats as you can so they don't feel too left out. Also, keep your cats' feeding schedule as close to their pre-baby schedule as possible. If you can't, make changes slowly and before the birth of the baby to give your cats some time to get used to any disruption.

Cat Walk

One way to give your cat some fresh air and exercise is to take her outside on a leash. One safe way to do this is to use a figure-H halter or figure-9 harness, with one strap that passes around your cat's neck and another strap that fits around her body behind the forelegs. Look for a harness that fits securely but isn't too constricting. If it's too tight, you can choke your cat, and if it's too loose, your cat may attempt to back out of the harness.

Some people prefer longer leashes; this is a judgment call. The advantage of a shorter leash—5 to 7 feet (1.5 to 21 m)—especially one with a handle that hooks around your wrist is that if danger threatens, you'll have faster access to your cat. If you decide to take your cat outside, first scout the area very carefully. Make sure you have a game plan ready for dealing with other animals you might encounter during your walks.

Children should be taught from an early age the proper way to handle and treat cats.

Bringing Home a New Cat

Moving to a new home and leaving a breeder or shelter, is as stressful for a cat as it is for a human. When you combine this with being forced to interact with one or more species of animals, you get a good sense of how a cat must feel being thrust into an unknown situation. He must feel overwhelmed by the new smells, sights, and sounds. You can help by giving your new cat some quiet time in a special room all his own at first, regardless of how many animals and how many species your cat will have to live with. This will give him time to take it all in and absorb changes in small chunks. Take your time with introductions because if things go well initially, it will provide a setting for long-term harmony in your household.

Introducing a New Cat to the Resident Cats

If you get a chance to interact with your new cat before bringing him home, take a piece of cloth, such as a handkerchief or small washcloth, back and forth between the cats at home and the new cat. Make sure your house cats' scent is on the cloth by rubbing the cloth on your cats' cheeks. Then rub this on your new cat's cheeks to transfer the smell onto him. When you bring this cloth home, let your cats sniff it or lie on it. Cats are creatures of smell, so this will help them get used to the new cat before he even comes into the house.

When you bring your new cat home, confine him to a room for at least three to four days. During this time, take bedding used by your other cats into the new cat's room, and any material he has had contact with to the other cats. After he has had a chance to lie in the other cats' bedding, take it back out. This way, the smells intermingle, and the new cat becomes a less foreign an entity.

After the smells from outside and inside have intermingled, bring the new cat outside in his carrier and allow the other cats into his room. Close the door to the new cat's room and let the new cat wander around the house without fear of attack. After half an hour to an hour, your new cat

Cats form close bonds with their feline siblings and create their own hierarchy.

will be ready to retreat to his familiar room, so take him back to his room and bring out the other cats, who will be just as ready to return outside and will be bursting with curiosity about what's been going on in their absence.

With each passing hour, you should start to see both the new and resident cats show interest in each other. This curiosity is perfectly normal; let them sniff each other while keeping the door to the room slightly ajar. Depending on how aggressive you feel any of the cats are, you can keep the new cat in his carrier or let him roam free in his own room while the door is slightly ajar. Keep a very close eye on all cats because they can move quickly and hurt each other in a split second. If you sense latent aggression in any of the cats, continue to take things slowly and not rush assimilation.

Cats often greet each other by nuzzling their faces. The highest compliment is when a cat gives someone a "bunt" with his forehead.

Cats and dogs can co-exist quite happily, provided proper introductions have been made.

If this interaction goes well, with only a little hissing but no spitting or growling, you can introduce one cat at a time to the new cat. Stand watch so you can intervene if one cat starts to attack the other. Introduce only one cat at a time to the newcomer so he doesn't feel ganged up on by several incumbent cats in the house.

Kittens are usually easier to assimilate into a home because they're perceived as less threatening by the resident cats. Kittens accept the fact that they're rather low on the totem pole and seem to take this in stride. They have very little fear and virtually no inhibitions, which makes them quite difficult for even the most curmudgeonly older cat to resist. Kittens are irrepressible little furry bundles of energy that older cats soon fall in love with, despite their best efforts.

When bringing home a kitten, pay much more attention to the resident cats and less to the kitten to keep your cats' jealousy at bay. For all these reasons, you can keep the isolation period shorter for kittens.

Introducing Cats to Dogs and Birds

Keep in mind that you can't trust all dogs around cats, nor can you trust all cats around birds. Even the most mild-mannered dog's prey instinct can kick in and take you and your cat by surprise, so be ready to monitor all interactions between cats and dogs and cats and birds for a long time, if not always.

A lot of cats, birds, dogs, and other animals live together happily in peace and harmony, so it's possible for this to occur in your household as well. All the basic rules for introducing cats to each other also apply to interspecies introductions. As with cat introductions, keep the new cat in a separate room and rub a cloth on the dog, which you can then allow your cat to sniff. After a few days of keeping the cat and dog separated, keep the dog on a leash while you open the door to the cat's room.

Let the cat approach the dog at his own pace. Some cats will immediately begin to sniff the dog's face and body, so keep a close eye on your dog at all times. If the cat appears calm and unafraid, you can allow the dog to approach him slowly. Keep the introduction short. Once the cat and dog have had an opportunity to sniff each other, separate the animals again.

If the cat and dog show an interest in meeting each other again with no sign of aggression on either's part, repeat the procedure you used in the first introduction, but let it last a little longer. Slowly increase the time the cat and dog spend with each other, keeping the dog on a leash the entire time. Be patient, and be ready for this process to continue for several days, even weeks. Never leave the cat and dog unsupervised until you're absolutely sure they're used to each other and can maintain cordial interactions. Similarly, some cats accept birds in the home without showing any interest in them, but don't assume this will happen. You might have to keep your bird in a cage unless the cat is out of the room.

Helping a Scared Cat Adjust to His New Surroundings

When you first bring a new cat into your home, give him some space, and let him set the pace for interactions with you and the other humans in the house. Give him a safe room he can retreat to. Cats feel safe in carriers, so leave his carrier in the room so he can feel as comfortable as possible.

Ignore a cat's signal that he is angry, upset, or scared at your own peril. If you see a cat with hackles raised, he feels threatened. It's best to give him some space.

Each day, go into your new cat's room and just spend some quiet time in there. You can lie on the floor so you're close to his level. During this time, you can read or speak to him gently to help him get used to you. Don't force any interaction such as petting or cuddling. If he seems scared and runs off to hide, don't force him to come out from his hiding place. If he hisses at you, walk away. Never raise your voice or punish him in any way. Soon your cat will begin to feel more comfortable with you and his new surroundings, and you'll be rewarded for your kindness and patience.

How to Stop a Cat from Scratching Where He Shouldn't

For cats, scratching isn't only pleasurable, it's necessary to condition their claws, shed old layers of claw, and expose new sharper ones. Also, when cats scratch they have the opportunity to stretch their bodies. Because scratching leaves their scent behind, it's also a natural form of marking for cats.

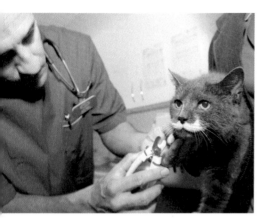

Regular claw-clipping will keep your cat comfortable and make him less likely to scratch inappropriately.

Indoor cats have no way to discriminate between acceptable and off-limit surfaces for scratching. To save yourself the aggravation of your cat destroying your furniture, drapery, and carpets, you'll need to develop strategies to help him scratch on appropriate objects.

The most important step you can take to prevent unwanted scratching it to give your cat a sturdy scratching post; make sure it's made of a different surface than your flooring or upholstery so you won't confuse your cat. If he has a scratching post made carpeting similar to what's on the floor, he'll treat them as one and the same and scratch either as the spirit moves him. Make sure the post is covered with material he can sink his claws into and remove without snagging them. Sisal, corrugated cardboard, and just plain wood bark are good options.

Next, make sure your cat has access to more than one post. Ideally, you should have scratching posts tall enough for your cat to get a good stretch in his muscles—at least 2 feet (0.6 m) high. Locate posts strategically throughout the house, close to the areas where your cat spends the bulk of his waking hours.

Encourage him to use the posts by spraying them with a catnip spray or hydrosol. You can also crush loose, dried catnip between your fingers and rub this all over the posts to attract your cat to the posts. When you see him scratching his post, praise him. Cats respond very well to positive reinforcement, and treats certainly don't hurt.

On the flip side, don't scold him when he scratches other areas. Some cats are deterred by squirt guns filled with plain water. Others seem oblivious to this and become quite adept at scratching when their people aren't looking. The key is to have your cat make a direct connection between the action and its consequence; otherwise, when you're not home to use the squirt gun, your cat will continue scratching. Although some people consider using water sprays and squirt guns cruel, it's preferable to declawing or finding a new home for your cat. If he responds without getting stressed out, squirt guns might be fine in certain situations.

If your cat keeps going back to a particular place in the house to scratch, such as a section of carpeting, first clean the carpet and backing thoroughly. Then, once the area completely dries, cover it with a piece of plastic or foil. Your cat will look elsewhere to scratch when he no longer has access to that area; you can use this opportunity to redirect his attention to his scratching posts.

Because most cats prefer scratching vertical surfaces, the tall, flat edges of your furniture are at most risk. If your cat starts to scratch furniture, cover it right away with a piece of foil covered with double-sided tape. Alternatively, you can cover the area with plastic wrap or contact paper, gummy side up, and secured in place with double-sided tape. The idea is for the feeling of this material on his paws to repel him and break the scratching-behavior cycle. If you don't do this, the scent his paws deposit on the surface will make him keep going back to the area. Keep the surface covered until your cat regularly scratches his post or horizontal scratching pad, as recommended in chapter one.

If your cat requires more persuasion that most, you can take steps to lessen the damage. The easiest option is to trim your cat's claws at least twice a month. This will cut down on scratching tremendously and, as discussed in chapter one, can be part of your cat's biweekly "spaw" routine. If trimming his claws doesn't deter your cat as much you'd like, you can apply a commercially available product over his claws, typically soft, blunt plastic sheaths you glue onto his nails. As your cat's nails grow, the sheaths fall off, and will need replacing.

Make your cat's scratching post more attractive by rubbing catnip on it or dangling toys from it.

Declawing

Most cat caregivers agree that cats should undergo certain procedures, such as spaying and neutering. Where cat lovers seem to part ways is over the subject of declawing. We advocate addressing issues such as scratching on carpets and upholstery without taking such an extreme, painful measure. Declawing has absolutely no benefit for a cat; it's done solely for the human's convenience.

Declawing is outlawed in most European countries as well as in Brazil, Australia, and New Zealand. In Canada and the United States, it's left to the discretion of veterinarians, who have to weigh their own

Never let a declawed cat go outside, as she is missing her primary means of defense.

ethical and moral views against the wishes of cat caregivers who simply want their cats to stop scratching inappropriately. It might help deter declawing if cat caregivers understood exactly what the process involves. Veterinarians and laypersons opposed to declawing view this as a surgery of convenience for the cat caregiver, and it falls under the same category as tail docking and ear cropping for certain dog breeds, only it's much more painful.

The technical name for a declawing procedure is onychectomy. Declawing literally means removing the claw and the bone from which the toes originate. It involves an amputation of each of the cat's toes at the last joint—the equivalent in humans of amputating just above the top joint the nail area of our hands or feet. Cats actively use their claws for playing, to balance while walking, and for other activities. Their claws are also their primary defense mechanism. Amputating part of the toe joint is a painful procedure that can have such long-lasting effects on a cat as lameness, trauma, and an inability to defend himself. Even barring painful complications from surgery, some cats have trouble climbing surfaces as a result of this surgery. Others become "biters" because they feel insecure without their claws.

The saddest situation of all is when a cat isn't even given a chance to prove himself and is declawed simply as a matter of course. Some may argue that if resident cats are already declawed, they couldn't protect themselves against a new cat armed with claws. This circular reasoning unfortunately results in all future cats brought into such a household being declawed, just because the first cat brought into that household was subjected to this procedure.

SURGICAL ALTERNATIVE TO DECLAWING

If behavior modification and claw trimming don't provide
results, another surgical alternative to declawing exists.
Tendonotomy, as the name suggests, involves removing the ten-
don that allows a cat to make grasping motions with his claws.
His claws will continue to grow and will need regular clipping to
prevent the claws from growing into the paw pads and causing
pain. His claws can also snag items and possibly get ripped out
if not cut to the appropriate length—up to but not at the quick.

 **You can teach
a cat to retract
his claws by gently
squeezing on the paw pad
when his claws are
exposed. Follow this up
with lots of encourage-
ment and treats.**

Although a tendonectomy cuts down on scratching because
a cat can't grip material and scratch the way he used to, consider how much
pleasure such a procedure takes away from him. Cats love scratching because
it allows them to stretch their claws, but a cat who's had a tendonectomy has
a harder time shedding his old claw sheaths and misses out on the stretching
action. Tendonectomies result in the same long-term problems as declawing
but have a shorter postoperative recovery time. If you can keep your cat's
claws trimmed and must go the surgery route, it's a somewhat better choice
than declawing in terms of pain during and immediately after the procedure.

Spraying or Inappropriate Elimination

Barring a physical problem, spraying or soiling outside the litter box is
almost always a dominance issue. It typically occurs as a response from your
cat to a territorial threat, either from inside the house, such as a new animal
or person, or from the smell or sight of an animal outside. The threat doesn't
have to be real; even a perceived threat can cause a cat to spray. Not just male
cats do this, although they tend to be more territorial; female cats also spray.

Male cats tend to mark vertical surfaces by standing with their tails
held vertical and stiff and backing up to an area while spraying urine. Male
cats large and small do this in the wild to define their domain and to deter
other males from entering their territory. It's a natural behavior for a cat that
makes the area smell more like himself, and thus more familiar and com-
forting. To help prevent this behavior, have your male cat neutered at or
before the first signs of sexual maturity. Once this behavior starts, it's more
difficult to control because the smell will keep your cat going back to the
marked area.

1. Signals a friendly happy cat
2. Tail is in neutral position
3. Do not provoke a cat with a wagging or thrashing tail because it signals that the cat is on high alert and that he is uncertain
4. Cats puff up their fur to appear larger than they are, so a feline with fluffed-up fur or a bottle-brush tail is prepared for imminent attack

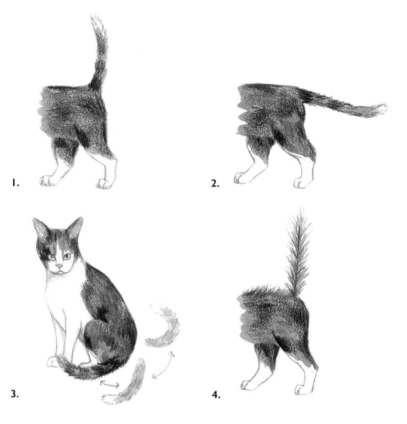

1.

2.

3.

4.

Nighttime or Early-Morning Crazies

Although people think cats are just nocturnal, thanks to domestication, today's house cat is more likely to be diurnal. This means they can stay awake during the day and sleep through part of the night. Cats need company, and if it can't be yours because you're sleeping, then another cat can really help alleviate boredom.

Provide interactive toys for your cat because if your cat sleeps all day, he'll in all likelihood want to play at night. Set aside a few minutes of playtime with your cat just before your bedtime. That way he'll get some attention from you and will work off some excess energy. You can follow play with a light snack to tide him over until morning and serves as a treat or reward, reinforcing playtime as something your cat will love.

If your cat still cries for attention or food very early in the morning despite this snack, disrupting your sleep, keep your door closed. If you can still hear them through the closed door, invest in a sound machine that plays white noise or nature sounds to will help drown out sounds and let you sleep through your cat's sounds.

Don't get up in the middle of the night or early in the morning and give in to your cat's demands, or you'll be rewarding unwanted behavior. Instead, set up a routine where you spend the quality playtime with them before bed and greet them with pleasure—and most importantly food—first thing in the morning. If your cat won't sleep in a special cat bed, get him some cardboard boxes, or give him access to his carrier.

If you have a particularly persistent cat, here's a sneaky way to help him associate unwanted early morning behavior with something negative: when he makes noise, turn on a noisy device he doesn't like just inside your door. Your cat will quickly make the connection between his activities and the noise. Cats particularly dislike vacuum cleaners, so they work well, although you'll have a hard time going back to sleep! Some cats don't like vacuum cleaners on sight, but others only get upset when one's turned on.

You can leave the vacuum cleaner, air cleaner, or other noisy machine outside your door with the switch in the "on" position. Then, you can plug it in from inside your bedroom to turn it on when you need it. Some extension cords have on and off switches that let you activate the appliance right from your bedside. Although this isn't a nice thing to do, it's extremely effective, and one or two days is usually all it takes for cats to take the hint. One or two days of not-so-nice behavior on your part will buy you years of peace and quiet, and you can then spend the rest of your time with your cat, showering him with love and affection to make up for this lapse.

Window perches or access to window sills can give house-bound cats a flavor of the outdoors.

Aggression, Mood Swings, and Unpredictable Behavior

Most aggressive behavior results from a perceived threat. For example, not all cats like being picked up, even by their "parents." Like humans, cats are individuals and have their own favorite ways of being handled. Some like to be held so they can grab onto and look over your shoulders, others like to be cuddled like a baby, and still others like to sit on laps but would rather not be picked up at all.

While it is not unusual for cats to engage in rough play, keep a close eye on the activity, as it can quickly escalate to aggression.

Aggression toward Other Cats

If another cat wanders into your yard, your cat will be able to smell him, even from inside, and will feel as if his territory is being invaded. Once the outside cat leaves, your cat will calm down and in all probability forget about it. However, if the outside cat continues to make his presence known, your inside cat will have a harder time. In such a situation, close the window coverings and coax your cat to play with you in a different part of the house. You can give him some catnip if it makes him happy. Let him take a whiff of a bottle of lavender hydrosol to calm him down.

Sudden Mood Shifts

Large cat statues, especially the ones with glowing eyes made from marbles, have been known to fool some cats into staying away from areas as well.

Sometimes cats will bite when they've had enough petting. What startles humans is that this reaction seems to come out of nowhere. But if you pay close attention, you'll begin to see a pattern: your cat will purr happily up to a point and beyond that point will suddenly get overly playful or bite. As you recognize this pattern, you'll learn to stop at the first warning sign.

Watch for your cat's ears to flatten against his head or a slight involuntary movement, or pay attention to your own sense that he's growing tired or becoming restless. At that point, don't force interaction; simply stop petting him. That will usually calm him down. Later, when he initiates it, you can have a short petting session again.

Tootsie Attack

Some cats love to hide and then attack an unsuspecting human's feet. This is just your cat showing off his hunting skills. You'll sometimes see cats stalk and pounce on each other as well. If cats don't have each other to practice their hunting skills on, they'll seek out the humans in the house. Anything that looks remotely like a prey animal or bird, such as the sash on a robe or a hand dangling by the side of the sofa, is usually fair game.

Playing with such toys as a shoelace tied to a wooden dowel and dragged along the floor or a dangling tie will give your cat a nice outlet for his hunting needs. Don't give your cat mixed signals, however; never offer your hand as something for him to attack or he'll consider it acceptable to play with your hand or other parts of your body, such as your feet. Use a pen, chopstick, or some other inanimate object if you want your cat to bat at something—never your fingers or hand.

Pet Peeves

Indoor cats are naturally apt to explore around the house. Sometimes they can get into trouble—for instance, if they jump onto a hot stove. Even if you don't have a problem with your cats walking on the counter, for his own safety, there are times it's best to keep him away from them.

Keeping Cats Off Counters and Other High Places

Even if you're careful not to leave such tempting foods as luncheon meat or fish on the counter, your cats may still find countertops irresistible. To deter them from jumping on counters, appliances, and furniture, don't scold them. Instead, rig up something that will surprise them to such an extent that they won't wish to repeat the experience. For example, you can place balloons, empty metal cans, or cans filled with pennies near the

Removing Urine Odor

If the spot is fresh, first blot it with paper towels, then pour either some white vinegar or plain seltzer water or club soda on the spot. Let the vinegar or club soda soak for about ten to fifteen minutes and then blot it up with absorbent towels or paper towels. If the urine has soaked through onto the backing of the carpet, your will cat likely to be able to smell the urine through the carpet and go back to that spot. If you can dry it all the way down, try and do so. If not, block access to this spot by covering it with some material your cat doesn't like, such as aluminum foil.

For older urine spots, if you can smell urine but can't pinpoint the exact area where your cat went, get a black light. You can find them at most hardware stores as well as at pet stores.

When you shine the black light on the suspected area, any urine stains will fluoresce. In some cases, club soda or vinegar might still do the trick for older urine stains, but in all likelihood neither will. In such a situation, a traditional home remedy used to remove skunk odors usually works well.

edges of counters so that your cats will knock them over when they jump on the counter. The loud noise will give your cats a rather rude surprise.

You can also place a sheet of contact paper, backing removed and sticky side up, or some double-sided tape on the counter. Your cats won't like the feel on their paws, and they'll think twice about jumping back up. If your cats are persistent, you might need to repeat this process for a few days. This method works because your cats will associate the negative experience directly with the act of jumping on the surface and so won't do this even in your absence.

Eating Plants

Some cats have an insatiable appetite for greens and enjoying digging and even munching on plants in your home or garden. Redirecting your cats to chew on something they like, such as catnip greens or wheat grass, can work quite well. Allow your cats access to these grasses so they eat these rather than chomp on your other plants.

Cats don't like citrus smells, so you can place dried or fresh orange or lemon peels or citrus soap slivers near your plants to deter your cat. If he seems to go after one particular plant, apply some cayenne pepper diluted with water on the leaves. This won't harm your plant but your cat

If your cats seem to enjoy eating greens, offer them some mesclun or other dark salad greens.

might not want to eat that plant again. You can also place chicken wire over the soil in your inside planters to keep cats from digging there. Pinecones, aluminum foil, or any sort of wire netting also works for this.

Outside, you can put chicken wire down in your garden and plant between the squares or diagonals. Cats will stay away from the chicken wire because it doesn't feel good on their paws. You can also turn on the sprinklers and surprise the cats with water. They won't like this, and won't want to return to that area.

Behavioral modification therapy—whether for scratching, digging in flowerpots, or jumping on surfaces—takes patience, love, and persistence. But you must balance this with how our cats' adorable, funny, and quirky behavior makes our lives so much richer. In the final analysis, we have to decide whether we're willing to take the time and make the effort to understand our feline companions rather

How to Keep Your Cat Gremlins from Attacking Toilet Paper

- Place a small paper cup full of water on top of the roll; most cats will be quite surprised—not to mention annoyed—to have water dumped on them.

- Balance a small aluminum can with ball bearings, pea gravel, or pennies on top of the roll so it makes a loud noise and startles them.

- Hang the toilet paper so it unrolls down the back toward the wall; that way, your cats can't just hold on to the top of the roll and pull it toward them to unroll.

- Purchase a commercial toilet roll cover; this rests on top of the paper roll and keeps the roll in place, which will prevent your cat from playing with it. You can make your own by slitting the cardboard core from an empty toilet paper roll lengthwise and placing it over the new roll. Make sure not to let much paper hang out from the slit or a playful cat will think it's a toy and attempt to pull it out.

- If none of the above tricks works, keep the bathroom door closed.

than looking for easy solutions that might not be the best choices for our cats. Sometimes all it takes is making that initial effort, and everything else will fall into place.

Conclusion

As our cats' guardians, it is up to us to make sure that their unique physical and psychological needs are taken into account when making decisions regarding their care. The message of this book is that this task is neither difficult nor complicated. Their brilliant eyes, soft shiny coats, and playful energy are our reward for having done our part by focusing on proper nutrition and natural healing methods.

REFERENCES

Bell, K.L. 2000. Hydrosol aromatherapy for your favorite feline. *Cats and Kittens.* www.aromaleigh.com/aromaleighinc/hyd.html

Brand-Miller, J., Hayne, S., Petocz, P., and Colagiuri, S. 2003. Low-glycemic index diets in the management of diabetes: A meta-analysis of randomized controlled trials. *Diabetes Care.* 26:2261-67.

Budayova, E. 1985. Effects of sodium nitrite and potassium sorbate on *in vitro* cultured mammalian cells. *Neoplasma* 32: 341-50.

Burger, I., ed. 1995. *The Waltham Book of Companion Animal Nutrition,* 2nd ed. Pergamon.

Case, L.P, Cary, D.P., and Hirakawa, D.A 1995. *Canine and Feline Nutrition.* St. Louis: Mosby.

Dierenfeld, E., Alcorn, H.L., and Jacobsen, K.L. 2002. Nutrient composition of whole vertebrate prey, excluding fish (fed in zoos). *Nutrient Advisory Group Handbook.* www.nal.usda.gov/awic/zoo/WholePreyFinal02May29.pdf

Ernst, M.R., Klesmer, R., Huebner, R.A, and Martin, J.E. 1961. Susceptibility of cats to phenol. *J Am Vet Med Assoc.* 138:197-99.

FDA guide to interpreting pet food labels. www.fda.gov/cvm/index/consumer/petlabel.htm

Goldstein, M. 2000. *The Nature of Animal Healing: The Definitive Holistic Medicine Guide to Caring for Your Dog and Cat.* Ballantine Books.

Hamilton, D. 1999. *Small Doses for Small Animals: Homeopathy for Cats and Dogs:* Berkeley, Ca: North Atlantic Books.

Hill, A.S., Werner, J.A., Rogers, Q.R., O'Neill, S.L., and Christopher, M.M. 2004. Lipoic acid is 10 times more toxic in cats than reported in humans, dogs or rats. *Journal of Animal Physiology and Animal Nutrition* 88(3-4):150-56.

Holistic cat care. www.holisticat.com

Morris, M., Lewis, L., and Hand, M. 1990. *Small animal clinical nutrition III.* Topeka, Ks.:Mark Morris Associates. my.execpc.com/~mjstouff/articles/vinegar.html

Ogilvie, G.K. 2002. Nutrition and cancer: Exciting advances for 2002 *Proceedings, World Small Animal Veterinary Association.*

Pitcairn, R. and Pitcairn S. 2005. *Dr. Pitcairn's Complete Guide to Natural Health for Dogs & Cats, 3rd edition.* Rodale Press.

Sptize, A.R., Rogers, W., and Fascetti. 2003. Supplementation with taurine can improve taurine status. *Journal of Animal Physiology and Animal Nutrition.* 87:251-61.

Thomas, J., Glatt, B., and Dierenfeld, E.S. 2004. Proximate, vitamins A and E, and mineral composition of free-ranging cotton mice *(Peromyscus gossypinus)* from St. Catherines Island. *Georgia Wiley InterScience* 23:253-61.

Ugarte, C., Guilford, W.G., Markwell, P., and Lupton, E. 2004. Carbohydrate malabsorption is a feature of feline inflammatory bowel disease but does not increase clinical gastrointestinal signs. *The American Society for Nutritional Sciences* 134:2068S-71S.

White, H.L., Freeman, L.M, Mahony, O., Graham, P.A., Hao, Q., and Court, M.H. 2004. Effect of dietary soy on serum thyroid hormone concentrations in healthy adult cats. *Am J Vet Res.* 65(5):586-91.

Willett, W., Manson, J., and Liu, S. 2002. Glycemic index, glycemic load, and risk of type 2 diabetes. *Am J Clin Nutr* 76:274S-80S.

Zoran, D.L. 2002. The carnivore connection to nutrition in cats. *Journal of the American Veterinary Medical Association* 221(11)

RESOURCES

Meat Farms

Several meat farms supply whole animals as well as whole animals ground with the bone included. When the meat arrives, it will have been in a cooler for a day or so, and in some cases, will be partially thawed. If you wish to add a little fiber to your cat's diet, you can mix to this ground meat some pureed or ground vegetables (2 tablespoons [28 g] per pound [455 g] of ground meat) as well as any supplements. Once you add water or meat broth, you'll find it provides for a lot more food than at first glance. You can store this mix in containers in the freezer and serve it slightly warm or at room temperature. At each meal, add 100 to 200 mg of taurine, unless you added it to the mix before freezing.

Wholefoods4pets
Located in Washington state; sells whole ground meats.
www.wholefoods4pets.com/dogs-cats.htm

Hare-today
Located in Pennsylvania; sells an excellent and large variety of raw meats.
www.hare-today.com

Big Creek Farms
Small farm in Tennessee with various meat choices; ships nationally.
www.bigcreekfarms.com

A Place for Paws
Based in Ohio; "Just Chicken" and beef as well as ground organs; can be customized.
www.aplaceforpaws.com

Raw-Meat–Only Options

Feed these on a strictly short-term basis or your cat may develop serious problems from a calcium deficiency. Long-term, you would need to add calcium or bone meal and some veggies. To see how much calcium to add to a pound of meat, go to the USDA website at www.usda.gov

Raw Advantage
Pluses: all meat and organs are organic. Available at various e-retailers, such as:
www.onlynaturalpet.com

Country Pet
Pluses and minuses: available at Whole Foods, Wild Oats, and other local outlets; easy as a first step in trying out raw food; mix of various meat sources, so read the label carefully in case your cat is allergic to any of the meats in this formula.
shopping.netsuite.com/countrypet

Commercial Frozen Raw Meat Mixes

Wild Kitty Cat Food
Pluses: uses organic, free-range poultry; 90 percent meat in the mix; no added supplements
www.wildkittycatfood.com/index.htm

Nature's Variety
Pluses: more variety of meats, including lamb, rabbit, and venison; comes in patties or medallions; 5 percent vegetables; some added supplements, but not too many.
www.naturesvariety.com

Oma's Pride
Pluses and minuses: nice variety of meats, but 20 percent vegetables is high and can cause problems for some cats with digestive issues such as IBD
www.omaspride.com

Aunt Jeni's Homemade4Life
Pluses and minuses: offers four types of meats; 20 percent veggie, which is a tad high; does match up the bone with the meat source; has some added supplements you might not want, including kelp and grapefruit seed extract
www.auntjeni.com/homemade.htm

Bravo
Pluses and minuses: Bravo Blends is a good choice if you want a mix containing meat and veggies (vegetable percentage not known); Bravo Basics offers ground meat and bone that lets you add in veggies if you wish; food comes in 1, 2, 5, and 10 pound (0.45, 0.9, 2.3 4.6 kg) tubes
www.bravorawdiet.com

Steve's Real Food

Pluses and minuses: contains eggshell and bone-meal powders in addition to chicken frames as calcium source; not as good as using ground bone as the sole and primary calcium source; very few varieties of meats

www.stevesrealfood.com

Primal Pets

Pluses and minuses: Primal Grinds preferable to mixes because these contain ground meat, muscle, organs, and bone to which you can add veggies; meat is antibiotic- and hormone-free; grinds offered unknown

Available at Whole Foods and some pet food stores

Canadian Sources

Urban Carnivore

Pluses: patties made from whole ground animals; nice variety, and a lot of sales outlets in Canada

www.urbancarnivore.com

Primal Veterinarian Diets

Pluses and minuses: very interesting meat choices (bison and goat); high-quality meat; no veggies

www.primalvetdiets.com

Calli's Cusine

Pluses: 2.5 percent veggies; mentions whole chicken most likely includes ground bone; nice choice of meats; also has nice, healthy cat treats for bribes

www.calliscuisine.com/cat%20food.htm
(website lists retailers)

Other Foods

These commercially available food choices for your cats don't require you to handle or feed raw meat. You can mix or match from these.

- Dehydrated meat, organs, and bones

- All-meat canned products, which require the addition of a bone source and veggies

- Wet and dry commercial food without grains; balanced calcium-to-phosphorous ratio

Dehydrated Meat, Organs, and Bones

These are balanced unto themselves. You can crumble these over your cat's food as a bribe or feed as a meal with or without water; because cats need a high-moisture diet, giving water is always useful.

Wysong's Archetype and Stella and Chewy's Carnivore Crunch: These both contain meat, organs, bones, essential fatty acids, probioitcs, and enzymes. They're grainless and not heated at any stage of the production process; you can crumble these over any type of food because they're balanced unto themselves, or you can reconstitute by adding water and feed as a meal. A downside is that these can get quite expensive, especially if you have a multi-cat household.

All-Meat Canned Products

Wysong's Au Jus and Evanger's 100% Meat Classic line: It's important to keep in mind that these aren't balanced foods; they contain only meat, no bones. However, you can add taurine, calcium or bone meal, and a small amount of veggies to make these appropriate for long-term feeding. You can balance Au Jus by adding Wysong's companion product, Call of the Wild. Both these formulas are quite rich; they can cause digestive upset in some cats. You can purchase Wysong's locally as well as online. Some reliable e-retailers are:

www.onlynaturalpet.com

www.petfooddirect.com

www.waggintails.com

Evanger: Petfooddirect.com and sitstay.com carry Evanger's products, but check the manufacturer's website for other retailers because the 100 percent meat line is harder to find

www.evangersdogfood.com/dog/allmeat.html

Tripett: This product consists of cans of green tripe from lamb and beef marketed for dogs. If you can't get raw green tripe from the butcher, this is an acceptable option for cats if you feed it in very small amounts. It's not a great option because it contains garlic, and even without garlic, it might be too rich for some cats.

www.tripett.com

Wet and Dry Commercial Food Without Grains

Keep in mind that these brands still contains carbohydrates, but the source is either potato starch or some other non-grain food.

Grainless Canned Wet Food Brands and Varieties

Innova EVO canned
www.naturapet.com

Wellness (by Old Mother Hubbard)
www.oldmotherhubbard.com

Nature's Variety/Prairie
www.naturesvariety.com

Merrick
Keep in mind that the flavors California Roll and Southern Delight contain grain. Grainless Merrick flavors include Cowboy Cookout, Grammy's Pot Pie, New England Boil, Surf & Turf, Thanksgiving Day Dinner, and Turducken.
www.merrickpetcare.com

Natural Balance Venison & Green Pea Ultra Premium Canned Cat Food
www.naturalbalanceinc.com

You can purchase all four of these brands through various online stores, including

- **Only Natural Pet**
  www.onlynaturalpet.com

- **Pet Food Direct**
  www.petfooddirect.com

- **Waggin Tails**
  www.waggintails.com

- **SitStay**
  www.sitstay.com

Grainless Dry Food Brands and Varieties

Although dry food isn't a desirable option for cats, if you must feed kibble, these are the best choices. Always make sure your cats drinks a lot of water if they eat dry food, and try to switch to canned (preferably raw) if at all possible.

Timberwolf Organics Cat Food
This contains potato but no other veggies; it does have kelp, alfalfa, yucca, and lots of other ingredients not everyone thinks cats should eat. They claim that close to half the food (in weight) consists of chicken; if so, it's much better than many commercial foods.
www.onlynaturalpet.com/Timberwolf_Organics_Cat_Food_s/276.htm

Natural Balance Venison & Green Pea
This is a better choice because the other Natural Balance varieties do contain grains.
www.onlynaturalpet.com/Natural_Balance_Venison_Green_Pea_Dry_Cat_p/158041.htm

"Love Your Cat"
This food doesn't appear to be available at any other e-retailers at this time.
www.prettybird.com/analyses.html

Innova EVO
This is currently available at very few e-retailers and not always easy to find locally. Here's their Web address and another online source:
www.naturapet.com/display.php?d=inn-home
www.epetpals.com/cat_food.htm

Cat Condiments

Dried Bonito flakes, also known as katsuobushi or hanakatsuo, are available at Whole Foods and independent Asian markets, especially Japanese stores.

Gimborn Freeze Dried Beef Liver for Cats

www.thatpetplace.com
www.valleyvet.com

Beefeaters Freeze-Dried Liver is available at Petsmart stores, both their bricks-and-mortar stores and at their website: www.petsmart.com

Cloud Star Tricky Trainers
www.ferretstore.com

Vets Best Rewards
www.canadavet.com

Rosie's beef dust powder
www.petfooddirect.com

Cookie Cutters

Copper Gifts.com
www.coppergifts.com

Pheromone Products

Feliway spray and plug-in diffuser
(manufactured by Farnam)
Available at Wal Mart, Petsmart, and Petco

Meat Grinders

These two brands of small, household meat grinders
are identical, except for wattage. They are 110 volt;
have on/off and reverse switches; have fine, medium,
and coarse plates for grinding, and weigh around
16 pounds (7 kg). You can order the Northern Tool,
item 168620, with a 1,000 watt motor by calling
800-221-0516. The Tasin TS-108 Electric Meat
Grinder, with a 1,200 watt motor, is only available
online; try checking eBay.

Hydrosols

You can find hydrosols at the following websites:

Adriaflor
www.adriaflor.com

Flutterbye Aromatics
www.flutterbyearomatics.com/hydrosols.htm

From Nature With Love
www.fromnaturewithlove.com

Nature's Gift
www.naturesgift.com

Prairieland Herbs
www.prairielandherbs.com/hydrosols.htm

Quality Pet Supplies
Drs. Foster & Smith, Inc.
www.drsfostersmith.com

Bulk Herbs

You can get herbal extracts and capsules readily at
grocery and drug stores. Although bulk herbs from
Frontier available at natural grocery stores, other bulk
herbs can be ordered online. The following are
sources for bulk herbs:

Atlantic Spice Company
www.atlanticspice.com

Frontier Natural Products Co-op
www.frontiercoop.com

Glenbrook Farm
www.glenbrookfarm.com/herbs

Mountain Rose Herbs
www.mountainroseherbs.com

Wild Roots
www.wildroots.com

Colloidal Silver

Keep in mind that you might need to order
higher concentrations of colloidal silver from the
manufacturer.

Meso Silver (manufactured by Purest Colloids)

Sovereign Silver (manufactured by Natural
Immunogenics Corporation)

**Wellness Colloidal Silver and Ultra Colloidal
Silver** (manufactured by Source Naturals)

Homeopathic Remedies

These remedies are available at most natural grocery
stores. Some common brands include Boericke &
Tafel, Boyron, Hyland's, and Standard Homeopathic.

Colostrum

You can get colostrum from these sources. You can
get raw colostrum only from Organic Pastures in
California and Peaceful Pastures in Tennessee.

Source Naturals
www.sourcenaturals.com

Symbionic's New Life
www.symbiotics.com

Organic Pastures
www.organicpastures.com

Flower Essences

Bach Flower essences
www.bachcentre.com

Flower Essences Society (FES)
www.flowersociety.org

Australian Bush Flower Essences
www.ausflowers.com.au

Flower Essences Preserved Without Alcohol

If you wish to avoid alcohol, you can get alcohol-free flower essences from these sources:

Green Hope Farms
www.greenhopeessences.com

Morningstar Essences
www.morningstar.netfirms.com

Mountain Meadow Botanicals
www.mmbotanicals.com

Tree Frog Farm Flower essences
www.treefrogfarm.com

APPENDIX A:

EXAMPLE OF CALCIUM SUPPLEMENTATION CALCULATION FOR NOT-JUST-FOR-SUNDAY TURKEY RECIPE (PAGE 77)

These types of calculations were performed to create the Recipe Matrix in chapter three. Only if you vary the recipe significantly—for instance, adding no liver one week and a great deal the next—would you have to perform these calculations on your own.

Not-Just-For-Sunday Turkey Dinner

*Turkey tidbits (muscle and organs)	Calcium amount (in mg)	Phosphorous amount (in mg)
Ground muscle meat	59	708
Liver	5	279
Heart	2	60
Gizzards	139	139
Total	205	1186

To get the supplementation amount:

Multiply 1,186 mg (phosphorous) times 1.3 = 1,541.8 mg calcium.

Because there are 205 mg of calcium in the various turkey tidbits in your recipe, you only need add:

1,541.8 mg - 205mg = 1,336.8 mg of calcium

If you add 1,336.8 mg of calcium, your turkey mix will have a calcium-to-phosphorous ratio of 1,541.8/1186 = 1.3:1.

*To perform calculations such as the above for other meats, obtain the calcium and phosphorous amounts for each part of the meat you're using. You can find this information at the United States Department of Agriculture website: http://www.nal.usda.gov/fnic/foodcomp/search

Add up the amounts in the calcium and phosphorous columns, and add between 1.2 and 1.4 times the phosphorous amount in the form of calcium powder.

APPENDIX B:
INFECTIOUS DISEASES

Regular veterinarian visits and a healthy diet help boost your cat's immune system, but infectious diseases can affect even the most well cared-for cats. This appendix outlines therapies for cats affected with the three most common infectious diseases: feline leukemia, (FeLV), feline immunodeficiency virus (FIV), and feline infectious peritonitis (FIP). Keep in mind that vaccinations should only be given to healthy animals, based on manufacturer and veterinary recommendations. If you have a cat that has tested positive for any infectious disease or is otherwise ill, never allow her to be vaccinated.

FeLV

How it's acquired: Feline leukemia spreads through saliva, blood, urine, and feces. All cats exposed to FeLV don't become infected, just as all humans exposed to cold viruses don't necessarily develop a cold. Mother cats can also pass on the virus to their kittens. Often, the disease isn't discovered until later in a cat's life when the immune system becomes impaired for some reason, such as stress or illness, and the latent virus particles become active.

Symptoms: Cats with FeLV tend to be prone to chronic illnesses. Depending on the cat, this can take the form of skin or eye problems; respiratory disease; infections in the mouth, gums, or tongue; frequent UTIs; and general digestive problems.

Testing: The ELISA antigen blood test detects FeLV. Because a single ELISA test isn't definitive, if your cat tests positive, you should have the ELISA repeated in three months. If you don't want to wait three more months to find out if your cats test positive, ask your veterinarian about a test called an immunoflurescence assay (IFA), which looks at the WBC count.

Vaccinations: A cat with FeLV shouldn't receive vaccinations; he already has a compromised immune system, and vaccines will further depress his immunity and cause disease. The FeLV vaccine is a killed vaccine that hasn't been established as particularly effective; its biggest drawback is its association with aggressive sarcomas that develop at the injection site.

Treatment: It's important to keep an FeLV cat's immune system strong and functioning well so they can fight off infections and diseases. Depending on your cat, you can crush supplement tablets and squirt soft gels into his food, or you can put all his supplements into one or two small capsules to cut down on the number of pills he must take. When shopping for cat-friendly supplements, look for minimal fillers and preservatives.

Supplements: As with any medicines, occasional breaks from herbs and supplements for a day or two can be a good thing. To prevent interactions, make sure your cat isn't taking any allopathic drugs when you give him these supplements.

For asymptomatic cats, you can give vitamin supplements and a well-formulated multivitamin capsule (look for one with minimal fillers). Or you can give:

- vitamin A: 1,000 IU daily
- vitamin B12: 250 mcg daily in methylcobalamin form
- vitamin B complex: 2.5 to 5 ml daily
- vitamin E: 100 to 200 IU daily
- vitamin C: 250 mg daily; adjust if your cat develops stomach upset; keep in mind that calcium ascorbate is easier on the stomach than ascorbic acid

Other supplements you can give your asymptomatic cat include:

- coenzyme Q10: 10 mg daily per 3 pounds (1.4 kg) of body weight; this helps with gum problems
- raw thymus glandular tablets: 200 to 250 mg daily
- 100 percent pure aloe vera juice with no sodium benzoate: 3 cc daily

Herbs: Tinctures are ideal because they contain the largest amount of the medicinal qualities found in an herb, but you can use the powder inside capsules. A maintenance dose of one capsule a day works well.

You can give it in one meal or spread it out in two meals each day. If you use alcohol-based tinctures, you can add 2 tablespoons (28 ml) of just-boiled water for each drop of tincture, and let sit in an open glass container. After the water has cooled and the alcohol evaporated, you can give 3 to 5 cc of this liquid each day.

You can give your cat either *Echinacea purpurea* or *Echinacea angustifolia*, or you can instead give *Astragalus* root. Most brands of both these herbs contain around 400 to 500 mg per capsule; a little variance in amount shouldn't make a difference. Because both these herbs are immune boosters, you can give the body a change of pace by giving echinacea for a month and then switching to astragalus the next month, or rotate them even more frequently than that.

In addition, you can give your cat shiitake mushrooms *(Lentinula edodes)* 500 to 600 mg, or one fresh mushroom per day; you can also buy this inexpensively in dry form and soak it in cold water, then puree and mix it in your cat's food. You can puree one dried mushroom and feed it over a four-day period.

If your cat catches an upper respiratory virus, start him on 250 mg of olive leaf extract immediately. Give it for at least fourteen days to help support his body. Olive leaf extract can thin the blood, so avoid this if your cat is on blood thinners.

For cats who begin to show symptoms of FeLV—*not* for routine maintenance—you can give the following herbal formula. It's a strong formula, and shouldn't be used in cats with kidney problems and used with caution in cats with diabetes. Many commercially available versions of this formula exist; don't purchase the ones that add kelp or red clover because the latter isn't safe for cats and the former should be used with great caution because it can over stimulate the thyroid gland. All these formulas contain burdock root *(Arctium lappa)*, sheep sorrel *(Rumex acetosella)*, slippery elm inner bark *(Ulmus fulva)*, and turkish rhubarb *(Rheum palmatum)*. The dosage is 5 cc or ml of brewed tea twice a day. You can also ask your veterinarian whether Feline Interferon, Acemann, and Immuno Regulin may help your cat.

FIV

How it's acquired: This virus is transmitted through cat bites that usually occur during catfights, which is why your veterinarian may recommended that you isolate your FIV-positive cat from other cats. It's rare for common cat interactions, such as sharing food and water bowls or grooming, to cause transmission from one cat to another.

Symptoms: FIV impairs cats' immune systems, causing them to succumb to secondary infections or diseases. Cats with FIV are more susceptible to secondary diseases, particularly gum infections, and are prone to sudden bouts of diarrhea. Because of their weak immune systems, they have a harder time healing from wounds and from infections in general. Another cat with flulike symptoms might recover quickly, but these cats take much longer to bounce back. They're also more likely to be anorexic and weak.

Testing: As with FeLV, the two tests typically used to determine the presence of antibodies are IFA and ELISA. However, the Western Blot test, which is more expensive than the other two, is the only definitive test. A positive blood test for FIV simply means that the cat has been exposed to the virus. This test isn't completely reliable, especially for cats younger than six months. In these cats, a positive FIV test results from the detection of antibodies passed from an infected mother cat, but the kitten will frequently test negative six months later. Death in most FIV-positive cats typically results from system shutdown as their organs fail almost simultaneously.

Vaccinations: The FIV vaccine is a killed vaccine with a poor efficacy rate, and cats vaccinated with the FIV vaccine will test positive.

Treatment: Treatment should focus on building up cats' defenses by strengthening their immune systems. Cats with FIV usually have a bleak prognosis, but that's because most traditional treatments further suppress the immune system. However, gentle herbal- and supplement-based regimens may help increase survival rates in cats and give them a chance to live normal lives. The same treatment recommendations for FeLV apply to FIV.

FIP

How it's acquired: This autoimmune disease results from a respiratory virus called corona virus. However, unlike the other two viruses, which a blood test can detect, diagnosis for FIP is quite difficult. Many corona viruses exist, and a positive diagnosis could simply mean that your cat has been exposed to a respiratory virus, not that he has FIP. The only reliable test for FIP is an organ biopsy.

Symptoms: FIP can cause lesions to appear on a cat's retinas; the classic FIP symptom for the wet or effusive form of the disease is the buildup of fluid in the belly. If the fluid builds up in the chest, it can cause difficulty in breathing. The dry or non-effusive form of FIP also affects the abdomen or chest but doesn't produce fluid buildup. Unfortunately, the dry form can turn into the wet form. The dry form of FIP is harder to diagnose than the wet form and can affect any organ system. How FIP will affect a given cat varies because it attacks different organs depending on the cat's susceptibility. If it affects the liver or kidneys, it will manifest as liver or kidney disease; if it affects the eyes, the cat might become blind. Some cats with seizures actually have FIP as the underlying cause. Most FIP diagnoses are made in either in kittens or in cats that have reached around ten years of age and have started to develop health problems as their immune systems weaken.

Testing: Clinical signs along with high blood protein levels, a high WBC count, and a positive corona virus antibody test are most likely to provide a definitive diagnosis. Unfortunately, your cat will need three different blood tests to obtain these results, so diagnosis can be quite costly.

Vaccinations: Infected cats should never be vaccinated.

Treatment and preventive measures: Treatment for FIP doesn't involve strengthening the immune system because the immune system overreacts and attacks itself. A better approach is to try and regulate the immune system. Allopathic treatment for FIP involves the use of cortisone, which can suppress the immune system. An intranasal vaccine for FIP has a 50 percent efficacy rate. Ironically, this vaccine isn't safe to give to kittens under sixteen weeks of age, so kittens most likely to benefit can't take this vaccine.

You can try giving your cat gentle massage around his heart area, where the thymus gland, which modulates the immune system, is located. You can also use just the tips of your fingers to give your cat five to ten gentle thumps daily on his chest to stimulate the thymus gland.

Supplements: The following supplements may help with FIP:

- either one thymus glandular tablet daily or raw organ meats, especially thymus gland and sweetbreads mixed into your cat's food, whether you feed commercial food or a raw diet

- $1/8$ to $1/4$ teaspoon (0.6 to 1.2 g) bee pollen per day

- $1/8$ teaspoon (0.6 g) digestive enzymes such as *Acidophilus* per day mixed in food

- $1/8$ teaspoon (0.6 g) vitamin C in powder form mixed into goat's milk yogurt or milk

- barley, rye, or wheat grass pureed in a food processor and added to food

FELINE UPPER RESPIRATORY TRACT DISEASE

A broad category of viruses, including the herpes and calici viruses, fall under the umbrella term of feline upper respiratory tract disease, commonly known as the cat flu.

Symptoms: Similar to the human flu, symptoms include sneezing, discharge from the eyes and nose, inflammation of the lining of the eyes (conjunctivitis), and loss of appetite, mostly because of a diminished sense of smell. Sometimes mouth and eye ulcers, fever, malaise, and excessive salivation accompany these symptoms.

Testing: The polymerase chain reaction (PCR) test is one of the few tests for this disease.

Vaccinations: None

Treatment: As with the human flu, feline respiratory illnesses result from viruses and require treatment. Although a healthy cat can get over these symptoms in a few days, a cat with a weak immune system can develop a secondary upper respiratory infection (URI). Left untreated, feline upper respiratory tract disease and URI can progress quickly and even be fatal in a cat with a severely compromised immune system. It's safest to assume the worst and support your cat's body with gentle therapies to help him recover from a virus. Your cat may need antibiotics if he develops an infection, but you shouldn't routinely use an antibiotic without confirmation of an infection. It can even lead to antibiotic resistance in the future, so use antibiotics judiciously.

Immediately isolate a cat with flulike symptoms from other cats in the household to prevent transmission. Use precautions, such as washing your hands frequently in warm water for thirty seconds, after handling an infected cat. After your cat has recovered from his upper respiratory illness, wash his bedding in hot water.

Calici and herpes

Calici and herpes viruses can cause recurring mouth ulcers and, in the case of calici, can sometimes cause a fever. Rhinitis-like symptoms, such as weepy eyes, accompany both viruses. Calici typically causes more nonrespiratory symptoms, such as stomach and even motor problems (sometimes called "lame kitten syndrome.") There is a calici nosode but not one for herpes. All the symptoms typically respond to treatment and shouldn't cause lasting damage with proper care and treatment.

Unfortunately, cats that recover from the herpes and calici virus tend to become carriers and shed the virus throughout their lives, particularly in times of stress. If your cat has a flare-up of symptoms, 500 mg of the amino acid L-lysine works very effectively. Cats need the amino acid arginine, but because lysine and arginine compete with each other, don't exceed a maintenance dose of 250 mg on a long-term basis. If your cat only has occasional symptoms, give L-lysine only when needed in the most conservative dose of 250 mg, and increase it to 500 mg only for short periods of time.

Externally, wash your cat's eyes with warm eye compresses and wipe away any discharges by soaking gauze or a small washcloth in warm water. You can add a few drops of lavender hydrosol to the water to help lift your cat's spirits. You can also use undiluted colloidal silver in the eyes and nose. Look for

concentrations under 150 ppm from a reputable manufacturer, such as one of the manufacturers listed in the Resources section of this book.

Internally, using the following herbs, supplements, and homeopathic treatments at the very first signs of a "cold" can be very effective:

Herbs

- stinging nettles: one capsule per meal mixed with food
- elderberry (without fruit and other artificial flavorings): one capsule per day
- olive leaf extract: one to two capsules per day
- *Andrographis paniculata* (an ayurvedic herb sold under many names, including Kolo Kare and Kan Jang): one pill per day
- propolis tincture: two drops per day with the alcohol boiled off in warm water
- grapefruit seed extract: one pill a day if you suspect the illness is likely to turn into an infection or in the very early stages of an infection

Supplements

- L-lysine: 500 mg for up to a week
- bovine colostrum: $1/4$ teaspoon (1.2 g) of powder mixed in with goat's milk, water, or food; particularly effective for orphaned kittens

Homeopathy

Aconite given at the very first signs of a respiratory problem can stop a cold dead in its tracks.

ACKNOWLEDGMENTS

Without the encouragement of my husband, I would never have considered taking on a venture as ambitious as writing this book. My thanks to John and to my friends for their continued love, support, and indulgence.

One of the best things about moving to Virginia has been meeting Dr. Schwabe. It has been wonderful to have a holistic veterinarian to help care for our cats. I am also greatly honored that she agreed to review my book and write a foreword for it. A great deal of the quality of the work is due to her, but any mistakes are mine.

Many thanks as well to my wonderful editor and fellow vegetarian Candice Janco, who hung in there with me through my holistic babble and talk of raw-meat diets.

No cat book would be complete without acknowledging the centers of our universe—these special furry creatures called kitty cats. My deepest thanks to my darling cats, angels Boo Boo, Tasha, and Hunny Bunny, as well as the current Fab Four who share my world: Trikki Tikki Tabbi, Pigpen, Missy, and Puma.

Last but not least, I want to express my appreciation to the wonderful supportive members of my online cat community on the *Holisticat* mailing list, many of whom I have known since 1997. I cherish you all, and share your deep love for cats.

PHOTOGRAPHER CREDITS

Mary Aarons, 88

Sandy Arora, 180

Rochelle Bourgault, 152

Courtesy of Drs. Foster & Smith, Inc./www.drsfostersmith.com, 13; 14; 15; 20; 22; 87; 105; 145; 154; 159

Betsy Gammons, 103

Regina Grenier, 143; 144

Rick Mitchell, 160

Allan Penn, 18; 34 (top); 42; 56; 57; 78; 80; 116; 118; 122; 124

Lisa A. Pierson, DVM, 70 (top)

Pat Price & Paul Deans, 83; 165

Nick Ridley/www.nickridley.com, 7; 8; 10; 21; 28; 35; 90; 91; 99; 101; 106; 133; 158

Linda Story, 5 (right)

Wother/www.jupiterimages.com, 62

Irina Yartseva, 4 (left); 167

ABOUT THE AUTHOR

Sandy Arora has devoted the last nine years of her life to helping people feed their cats a species-appropriate diet, and treat their cats' health using gentle holistic means. Through her *Holisticat* mailing list on Yahoo and website holisticat.com, she has supported thousands of cat caregivers, and continues to give freely of her time. She resides in Virginia with her equally cat-crazy husband and their four fabulous felines. Sandy and John are passionate about cat rescue and despite their university teaching schedules, they find time to rescue cats and kittens in need.

ABOUT REGINA SCHWABE, DVM

Regina Schwabe, DVM is a practicing veterinarian with a special interest in holistic therapy including nutrition. A graduate of the Tieraerztliche Hochschule Hannover, Germany, Schwabe is certified in veterinary acupuncture and chiropractic care. Her practice has encompassed large as well as small animals, but is currently focused on integrative medicine for dogs and cats. Pamplin Animal Wellness Services is located in rural central Virginia.

INDEX